PRAISE FOR

GOD SPEAKS

As life inevitably takes each of us through sufferings similar to
that of Job, we will no doubt have questions similar to those Job
asked—"Where is God in all this?" "Why doesn't He deliver me?"
God Speaks gives answers, and with those answers comes much-
needed comfort.

KIRK CAMERON
Actor and Co-author of *Still Growing* and *Conquer Your Fear, Share Your Faith*

The storms of this life are inevitable, and we know from Scripture
that only those who build their house on rock will survive. *God
Speaks* lays out God's building plans through the gospel simply
and succinctly. It is the perfect gift for those who don't know the
Lord as well as for those who need comfort in tribulation.

TODD FRIEL
Host of *Wretched* Radio/TV

GW00730434

GOD
SPEAKS

FINDING HOPE IN THE
MIDST OF HOPELESSNESS

Life Lessons from the Biblical Book of Job

RAY COMFORT

Published by Regal
From Gospel Light
Ventura, California, U.S.A.
www.regalbooks.com
Printed in the U.S.A.

Library of Congress Cataloging-in-Publication Data
Comfort, Ray.
God speaks : finding hope in the midst of hopelessness / Ray Comfort.
pages cm
Includes bibliographical references and index.
ISBN 978-0-8307-6624-6 (trade paper : alk. paper)
1. Bible. O.T. Job—Criticism, interpretation, etc. I. Title.
BS1415.52.C66 2013
223'.106—dc23
2013006501

Rights for publishing this book outside the U.S.A. or in non-English languages are administered by Gospel Light Worldwide, an international not-for-profit ministry. For additional information, please visit www.glww.org, email info@glww.org, or write to Gospel Light Worldwide, 1957 Eastman Avenue, Ventura, CA 93003, U.S.A.

To order copies of this book and other Regal products in bulk quantities, please contact us at 1-800-446-7735.

This book is dedicated to Lori Nason. She was a passenger in a car that was hit by a drunk driver in 2007. The accident put her into a coma for three weeks and also caused her to have a stroke. Her injuries included a broken hip, pelvis, leg, collarbone and sternum, broken ribs and a collapsed lung. Lori also lost one of her breasts. Lori had been a freelance writer, but even after five years of rehabilitation, her ability to write remained stolen by the stroke. Her world came crashing down in an instant of time, and she found herself in the despair of a Job experience. May this book give her and others in troubling situations comfort beyond words.

CONTENTS

INTRODUCTION

Although we try to fortify ourselves against the storms of life, trials and difficulties are virtually unavoidable. However, the book of Job contains comfort beyond words—it offers remarkable knowledge and wisdom of which this pain-wracked and suffering world knows nothing.

When we suffer, we usually want to know why bad things are happening to us. But the comfort we find in the book of Job does not come from finding out *why* we suffer but rather in coming face to face, as did Job, with a holy and just God.

Job's servants were murdered, his possessions stolen, his children killed and his health taken away. Job lost everything but his faith in God and a stubborn desire to have a personal audience with the Almighty. He wanted to ask the Lord why such terrible suffering had come his way—to talk face to face with his Creator.

When he finally got that personal audience, God didn't answer even one of Job's questions. Instead, He had 70 of His own to ask Job. But Job wasn't disappointed. Neither will we be disappointed if we take the time to study Job's story of grief and loss and God's responses to this suffering man. *God Speaks* draws from the book of Job, a book in which are hidden amazing truths—including scientific truths that were not discovered in this world until more than 3,000 years later—that prove the trustworthiness of Scripture.

As we look into the Word of God through the story of Job, may it enable us to look past our problems and to rest in the faithful God who is revealed in its words.

GOD
SPEAKS

JOB AND TRAGEDY

Job 1:1-22

Who was the greatest man who ever lived? Was it Socrates, Lincoln, Gandhi, Beethoven, Shakespeare, Leonardo da Vinci? All these men were great, but Jesus said that the number one was John the Baptist. He said there was none born of women who was greater than John. John didn't invent anything, or paint masterpieces, or write astute plays. He did, however, stand against evil, and like Lincoln and Gandhi, he was murdered for what he believed.

It seems that if John were the greatest, then God would not have allowed him to be cut off in his prime. The Lord could easily have stayed the hand of the executioner, but He didn't. He could have opened the prison doors for John as He later did for Peter, but He didn't. Why didn't God do a miracle for His number one? One thing we do know is that we *don't know*. From a human perspective, intervention on John's behalf was certainly warranted, but for some reason there wasn't a peep from Heaven in his defense.

Perhaps coming in a close second on the list of great men is a man about whom most of the world has never heard. His name was Job, and he had a best-selling biography written about him, despite the fact that his story is about pain and suffering.

We all try to fortify ourselves against suffering, but each of us eventually proves to be like an aged house in a heavy rainstorm of trials. Suffering at one time or another rains down on us, and the constant drips keep coming through our ceiling, no matter how much we try to patch the roof.

Job's whole ceiling caved in. Few of us will suffer to the degree to which Job suffered, but his biography sets an example for us of how we can best handle our pain when life's sorrows and troubles overwhelm us. Job's story gives us a perspective on God's thinking.

The book begins with the ultimate foreword—an incredible character reference:

> There was a man in the land of Uz, whose name was Job; and that man was blameless and upright, and one who feared God and shunned evil (Job 1:1).

Job was a sinner, like the rest of us, and he battled against his sinful nature. However, he was "blameless" (no doubt through the sacrificial system), and he was unique in that he feared God and rejected evil. He wasn't "born again" with a new nature, regenerated and helped by the Holy Spirit in his weakness as is the believer in Christ. Yet in his unregenerate state, Job shunned evil. That's amazing for a human being, as Jesus testified that we love the darkness and hate the light. We run toward sin as a moth flies to a flame.

The cynic may look at Job and say that there was a reason he shunned evil. Job had no reason to steal, as a poor person does, because he was rich. *Very* rich. He had no reason to covet anyone else's wealth, to be greedy or to be angry about life's realities. So half of the seven deadly sins that poor people have to battle were no problem for Job. Here's how rich Job was:

> And seven sons and three daughters were born to him. Also, his possessions were seven thousand sheep, three thousand camels, five hundred yoke of oxen, five hundred female donkeys, and a very large household, so that this man was the greatest of all the people of the East (Job 1:2-3).

Job was rich and powerful, and he was blessed with 10 healthy and happy kids. He had it made. However, the Scriptures pull back the veil over the supernatural world to give us a glimpse into the spiritual realm regarding Job's life. Here we see God Himself speaking about Job to the ultimate cynic:

> Then the LORD said to Satan, "Have you considered My servant Job, that there is none like him on the earth, a blameless and upright man, one who fears God and shuns evil?"
>
> So Satan answered the LORD and said, "Does Job fear God for nothing? Have You not made a hedge around him, around his household, and around all that he has on every side? You have blessed the work of his hands, and his possessions have increased in the land. But now, stretch out Your hand and touch all that he has, and he will surely curse You to Your face!"
>
> And the LORD said to Satan, "Behold, all that he has is in your power; only do not lay a hand on his person."
>
> So Satan went out from the presence of the LORD (Job 1:8-12).

Shortly after this glimpse into the supernatural, Job's life turned a corner. Job's children were celebrating in their oldest brother's house one day, and a messenger came to Job and told him that thieves had stolen his oxen and donkeys and had killed his servants. Then the messenger said, "And I alone have escaped to tell you!" While he was still speaking, another messenger arrived and told Job that his sheep and more of his servants had been struck by lightning and killed. Then he said, "And I alone have escaped to tell you!" While he was still speaking, a third messenger arrived and reported that Job's camels had been stolen and more of his servants murdered, and then the messenger said, "And I alone have escaped to tell you!" Then (believe it or not) while he was still speaking, another messenger came and told Job that his beloved children had been partying when a tornado had hit the house in which they had been sitting. All four corners of the house had collapsed and killed all his children. Then the messenger said (you guessed it), "And I alone have escaped to tell you!"

The Bible is full of . . . well . . . intellectually embarrassing situations, and this is one of them. This narrative sounds like some sort of four-men-came-into-a-bar joke or the beginning of a Grimm's fairytale. There are four disasters, and in each disaster only one person is saved. Each of these survivors finds Job and parrots the exact same sentence to him. For two servants to show up and say the same thing would be an amazing coincidence. Three would be a big stretch. But four is ridiculous—unless the story is found in the Bible. It's because this story is in Scripture that the dynamic radically changes. If something is in the Bible, we are no longer talking about a coincidence or a big stretch. We are talking about the supernatural.

Two Classes

The Scriptures speak of only two classes of people living on this massive earth: the natural person and the spiritual person. Natural people live and think in the realm of nature. They understand through their natural senses, and to them everything has a natural and rational explanation. For them, pigs don't fly, and people don't walk on water. Seas don't split apart and allow masses of people to walk through them. Snakes and donkeys don't talk, walls don't fall down when people shout, arks don't carry animals two by two, the blind aren't made to see with the touch of a hand, and the dead aren't brought back to life with a spoken word.

But the *spiritual* man or woman sees things very differently. For those who are spiritual, *anything* goes, because they are dealing with the supernatural. With God, anything is possible. Demon-possessed pigs can leap off cliffs, snakes and donkeys can talk, the deaf can hear, the blind can see—and what's more, nothing needs to be explained. God created natural law, and He can suspend His own natural law any time He wishes.

As a Christian, I don't wrestle with things like *whether or not* Jesus multiplied the bread and fish; I already believe that He did. But I do wonder *how* He did His miracles. Were the fish cooked? Were the multiplied fish identical to the original ones? Or when Jesus walked on the water, how deep did His feet sink into the water upon which He walked? Or when the children of Israel walked through the Red Sea, could they see fish in the walls of water on each side?

There's a reason that those who are born again never doubt the miracles of God. They have already experienced their own big miracle. The moment they repented of their sins, they came to know God; their eyes and ears were opened, and faith came to them as a gift from God. It's as though their lungs had been clogged with the filth of sin, and God had given them a lung transplant. Believing the Bible now comes to them as naturally as would breathing with a set of new and healthy lungs. A new life as well as times of refreshing came to them from the presence of the Lord (see Acts 3:20).

If you have not been born again (see John 3:1-21), you are a natural man or woman. You therefore have a few intellectual problems that make you gasp a little when it comes to the subject of God and the supernatural. Let me ask you some questions to see if I can pinpoint the trouble for you: What was in the beginning? What produced this huge, incredible natural world in which we live? If you say it was the Big Bang, then let me ask you where the materials to make the Big Bang came from? If the Big Bang was the product, who or what was its producer?

Sound, like that which we would hear in a loud bang, travels in waves, as do light and heat; but unlike light and heat, sound moves by making molecules vibrate. So for sound to travel anywhere, there must be molecules for it to travel in. On earth, sound travels to our ears by vibrating air molecules, but there are no molecules in space. Therefore there was no bang in space, because there are no molecules to vibrate. So if the Big Bang happened, it was more of a Big Silence. But what was it that caused this Big Silence to explode? You can't say that it caused itself, because for it to do so it would have had to exist before it existed to cause itself to explode. If it existed before it existed, then it wasn't the beginning, because it already existed. For something to create itself is scientifically impossible, of course, but common sense alone will tell us that such a thing cannot happen.

Many scientists now believe that there was "something" before the Big Bang, but they're not sure what it was:

> Ten years ago . . . there was no doubt that the Big Bang was the beginning. But today, the certainty has gone. There is no escaping the inconvenient truth that the Hubble's graph, work of genius though it is, contains a huge problem. It tells us that everything we see in the universe today—us, trees, galaxies, zebras, emerged in an instant, from nothing, and that's a problem. It's all effect, and no cause.[1]

It's only a problem if you reject God as being the first cause.

The solitary rational explanation for the origin of the universe is that something immaterial, eternal and unspeakably powerful created it. The source of this world had to be something *supernatural*. So you are forced to fall back on a belief in the supernatural, and in doing so, you are therefore saying that the impossible happened—that something supernatural created everything from nothing. A belief in the supernatural is much bigger than a mere belief in flying pigs. So if the supernatural had a hand in making birds, flowers, trees, fruit, horses, cows, elephants, milk, cheese, eggs and butter, it's only natural to believe in the supernatural as it is portrayed in the Bible.

Job 1 necessitates the supernatural. Whoever penned this book's 42 chapters was either supernaturally lifted into Heaven to witness and record the dialogue between God and Satan and then was able to listen to the conversation between Job and his three friends, or he was supernaturally given the material by divine revelation.

So, the supernatural book of Job is entirely in keeping with the rest of the supernatural Word of God. As with many other strange instances in Holy Scripture, the fact of four men coming to Job, each of them having nearly the exact same account, may be hard for some to swallow. But gnat-straining thoughts of doubt will only keep us from the comforting truths of Holy Scripture.

It is a freeing thing to be able to let go of doubt and rest in knowledge-based trust. It's like a man who has never flown in a plane letting go of his natural reasoning. He could sit in his seat indignantly mumbling that it is impossible for human beings to fly at 35,000 feet in the air at 500 miles per hour in a massive steal can with wings. On the other hand, he could say that air travel is a reality that he can't deny, and he could therefore relax; or he could reason a little and consider the way gravity can be superseded by the law of aerodynamics and that it is possible for a steel can to be airtight and filled with renewable air so as to keep human beings alive at that height.

You and I can rest in the fact that all of us who believe in a Creator of creation also believe in the supernatural; or we can have a knowledge-based trust that works things out a little by realizing that God has deliberately placed strange and hard-to-believe instances in the Scriptures in order to humble the proud. All who trust that the Bible is the Word of God are forced to humble themselves and become as little children, much to the scorn of a proud and godless world. But that is the way of salvation. The door has been made low to exclude those who are wise in their own conceits. God resists the proud and gives grace to the humble.

HIS FORTIFICATION

So how did Job handle the fourfold and terrible news? He didn't hold his fist to the heavens and accuse God of some sort of wrongdoing. The man tore his robe, shaved his head, fell to the ground and worshiped God. Job was a godly man. He knew that God is the giver of life and that ultimately He's also the One who takes life away. That was Job's fortification. Every blessing and every good gift comes from above.

But this isn't how the ungodly think. God isn't in their thoughts (see Ps. 10:4). Millions don't attribute the blessings of loved ones, food, light, the seasons, color, beauty, fruits, eyesight, hearing or their own lives to God. They think that human beings are the mere product of change. There was a big bang, and there you have it—we are here. No one is to be thanked for anything. Others believe in the existence of God, but they never even think to bow their heads in prayer and thank Him for His amazing kindness. Even though their very ability to breathe comes from their Creator, if you ask them what God has done for them, they will shake their heads and say, "I can't think of anything." I know this because I have asked many people that question. I also know it because I was once in darkness, alienated from the life of God through the ignorance that was in me because of the blindness of my heart.

But Job was different. He was insightful and thankful, even in his unregenerate state. Look at the humble words he spoke as his life was being torn apart:

> Naked I came from my mother's womb, and naked shall I return there. The LORD gave, and the LORD has taken away; blessed be the name of the LORD (Job 1:21).

Charles Spurgeon put these words of Job into perspective when he said:

> Job lost his ten children at a stroke. O Death, what an insatiable archer thou wast that day, when ten must fall at once! Yet Job says, "The Lord hath taken away." That is all he has to say about it: "The Lord hath taken away." I need not repeat to you the story of the gardener who missed a choice rose, but who could not complain because the master had plucked it. Do you feel that it is just so with all that you have, if he takes it? Oh, yes! why should he not take it? If I were to go about my house, and take down an ornament or anything from the walls, would anybody say a word to me? Suppose my dear wife should say to the servant, "Where has that picture gone?" and the maid replied, "Oh, the master took it!" Would she find fault? Oh, no! If it had been a servant who took it down, or a stranger who removed it, she might have said something; but not when I took it, for it is mine. And surely we will let God be Master in His own house; where we are only the children, He shall take whatever He pleases of all

He has lent us for a while. It is easy to stand here and say this; but, brothers and sisters, let us try to say it if it should ever come to us as a matter of fact that the Lord who gave should also take away.[2]

What wise and wonderful words! Job held onto the things of this world with a loose hand, and so must we if we want to bolster ourselves against inevitable suffering. Job's words need to be close to all our hearts, because his experience could happen to any of us in a moment of time. Every day we hear of lives being torn apart by bombs, tornados, hurricanes and accidents, and the attitude that was Job's must be the attitude that is our own fortification and consolation. We are mere custodians of our loved ones. They belong to God, as He is their Creator.

A friend of mine once told me that he'd had a terrible morning. His car had broken down, and he'd had to go to the expense of renting a vehicle to get to work and to deal with the hassle of getting his own car repaired. But then his eyes lit up with joy as he told me that he had bumped into a man at the repair shop who had listened intently as my friend Scotty had shared with him the gospel. God had prepared the man for this conversation. My friend was convinced that it was a divine encounter, and that knowledge made him feel that the morning's hassle made sense.

Often the Christian doesn't have to look too far to see God's hand in life's trials. God promises to work all things for the good of those who love Him and are called according to His purposes (see Rom. 8:28). But it is also true that we do not always recognize God's hand in our trials or see what good purpose could come of them. So I, in semi-jest, cynically responded to my friend Scotty, "So what was the purpose of Job's experience as he sat in misery, covered with boils from the crown of his head to the sole of his feet? Was he holding a gospel tract and looking for some divine encounter?" I couldn't see too much light in Job's long and dark experience other than the divine revelation that he was vile—and I knew that there were less painful ways for a person to gain that awareness.

Scotty smiled and said, "Are you kidding? *Millions* have taken comfort from Job's experience." It was a "duh" moment for me. It is true! Millions of people have found consolation in their sufferings *because of the book of Job*. The Maker of the universe looked into the future to the day when billions of copies of the Bible would be printed and bring light to those who would find themselves in terrible darkness. Job had no idea how much good would come from his terrible suffering. He didn't know that he would be admired and preached about and written about through the ages:

> My brethren, take the prophets, who spoke in the name of the Lord, as an example of suffering and patience. Indeed we count them blessed who endure. You have heard of the perseverance of Job and seen the end intended by the Lord—that the Lord is very compassionate and merciful (Jas. 5:10-11).

Job had no idea that he would become one of the greatest heroes of the best-selling book of all time, which would be published more than 3,000 years after his dreadful experience.

JOB AND EVIL

Job 2:1-10

Rob Brendle, founding pastor of Denver United Church and former associate pastor at New Life Church in Denver, Colorado, wrote the following about Rachel Works, a victim of the shooting at New Life Church that took place on December 9, 2007:

> Her family had come to a church where I was pastoring that morning, a routine Sunday. A thousand things would never have crossed their minds as they drove through Colorado Springs toward New Life Church's enormous concrete worship center—including the prospect of being assaulted in their minivan by a young man with a high-powered rifle.
>
> Later that day, we were all at a local hospital. The girl whose hand I held, Rachel, had already lost a sister at the scene. Her father was down the hall in critical condition and her mother was coming undone in the waiting room, but she didn't know any of it. Rachel lay unconscious for a couple of hours more in the ICU.
>
> And then she died. Her family had come to church together that morning, and by nightfall they were shattered.[1]

Modern prosperity preachers set up their followers for a fall when they use the Bible to promise health and wealth. We don't have to look too far to find Christians who are going through Job experiences. In a moment of time, the godly can lose savings, be involved in a serious car accident, be the victims of violent crime or get a terminal disease. This is not negative talk or the speech of unbelief. It is a biblical reality. We are not to live in dread of the future, but neither are we to live in a world of make-believe.

I know of a respected pastor of a large church whose precious wife has a serious case of Alzheimer's. He has lost the love of his life. He himself also has lung cancer. This pastor and his wife are both elderly, and barring a miracle, their future in this world looks very bleak. But their dark experience is working for their good (see Rom. 8:28).

They are going through a fiery trial today, and you and I may go through a fiery trial tomorrow:

> Beloved, think it not strange concerning the fiery trial which is to try you, as though some strange thing happened unto you (1 Pet. 4:12, *KJV*).

Jesus warned that the storms of this life fall on the just and the unjust:

> Therefore whoever hears these sayings of Mine, and does them, I will liken him to a wise man who built his house on the rock: and the rain descended, the floods came, and the winds blew and beat on that house; and it did not fall, for it was founded on the rock.
>
> But everyone who hears these sayings of Mine, and does not do them, will be like a foolish man who built his house on the sand: and the rain descended, the floods came, and the winds blew and beat on that house; and it fell. And great was its fall (Matt. 7:24-27).

The difference between the wise man and the foolish man is seen in whether or not their houses fall.

Everything good that we have comes from God—the rain, the sunshine, our health, our food, cute kittens, super-cute puppies, smiling babies, pure-white driven snow, deep-blue sea filled with tasty fish, cool water to drink, succulent fruit to eat, and fresh air to breathe: "Every good gift and every perfect gift is from above, and comes down from the Father of lights, with whom there is no variation or shadow of turning" (Jas. 1:17). However, instead of having a heartfelt thankfulness to God for all these undeserved blessings, this wicked world ignores God's will, blasphemes His name, kills unborn children, fornicates, commits adultery, glorifies pornography, mocks the Word of God, promotes homosexuality, despises the gospel, and says that evolution gave us all the blessings of life. But the irony is that when tragedy strikes, they intuitively remember God and ask, "What have I done to deserve this?"

JOB'S BELOVED WIFE

The truth is, the best of us are extremely sinful in God's eyes, and all of us deserve wrath and Hell. The only reason that we are still drawing breath is that God is good, kind and rich in mercy. Job knew this. Bible commentator Matthew Henry said of Job:

> The devil tempts his own children, and draws them to sin, and afterwards torments, when he has brought them to ruin; but this child of God he tormented with affliction, and then tempted to make a bad use of his affliction. He provoked Job to curse God. The disease was very grievous. If at any time we are tried with sore and grievous distempers, let us not think ourselves dealt with otherwise than as God sometimes deals with the best of his saints and servants. Job humbled himself under the mighty hand of God, and brought his mind to his condition. His wife was spared to him, to be a troubler and tempter to him. Satan still endeavors to draw men from God, as he did our first parents, by suggesting hard thoughts of Him, than which nothing is more false. But Job resisted and overcame the temptation.[2]

Tragedy struck the hardest of blows to poor Job. This man lost his servants, his wealth and his beloved children, despite the fact that he had so diligently sanctified his sons and daughters—such was his love and concern for their happiness. Now they were gone. Again, the Scriptures pull back the veil so that we have insight into the eternal:

> Then the LORD said to Satan, "Have you considered My servant Job, that there is none like him on the earth, a blameless and upright man, one who fears God and shuns evil? And still he holds fast to his integrity, although you incited Me against him, to destroy him without cause."
>
> So Satan answered the LORD and said, "Skin for skin! Yes, all that a man has he will give for his life. But stretch out Your hand now, and touch his bone and his flesh, and he will surely curse You to Your face!"
>
> And the LORD said to Satan, "Behold, he is in your hand, but spare his life."
>
> So Satan went out from the presence of the LORD, and struck Job with painful boils from the sole of his foot to the crown of his head. And he took for himself a potsherd with which to scrape himself while he sat in the midst of the ashes.
>
> Then his wife said to him, "Do you still hold fast to your integrity? Curse God and die!" (Job 2:3-9).

It's easy for us to vilify Job's wife as a shallow, godless, unfaithful woman who failed to be a helpmate to her beloved husband. But let's not be too quick to judge this poor woman. Like Job, her life had been picture perfect. She was rightly respected because of her social position alongside her esteemed hubby. She had borne 10 healthy children, and she was happy in the knowledge that her family's future was financially secure. Who doesn't want that for their kids? If anyone ever had God's blessing it was Job, his wife, and their 10 children. But then, in a moment of time, this woman's precious children were dead—all 10 of them. Whoever heard of such a tragedy!

Think of the mothers in Bethlehem, 2,000 years ago, whose children had been slaughtered by Herod simply because he was peeved that he had been deceived by the wise men (see Matt. 2:1-18). Scripture said that those grieving mothers refused to be comforted. No one could simply put an arm around these women and say, "God is in control. This tragedy will work for your good. It's okay."

Each mother had conceived a child in joy, carried it for nine months, birthed it in pain, and no doubt gloated over it with the delight that only a mother can know. Each of them had embraced, fed, nurtured and suckled her baby, listened to her child's first word and seen the baby's first stumbling step. In that culture these mothers would have looked deeply into the wide eyes of their children and heartily thanked God for such wonderful blessings. Children bring a joy to life to which nothing can compare. But suddenly, for no real reason, each of these little children felt the sharp and merciless Roman sword thrust through their soft flesh. The mothers of Bethlehem embraced their dead children, their trembling hands covered in blood! The sweetness of life had suddenly turned bitter, and according to Scripture, no amount of consolation could help these women rid themselves of grief. Multiply such grief by 10, and you have a taste of the bitterness of soul experienced by Job's unfortunate wife.

Perhaps Job's wife had been present as each of her precious children's crushed and bloodstained bodies had been pulled from the dust and rubble. No doubt she wailed in typical Middle Eastern fashion at such a sight and then wept until she could weep no more as each one of her beloved children was buried.

If at any time in her life Job's wife needed the love and support of her husband, it was now. But Job wasn't able to stand up and put his strong and loving arms around her to at least try to comfort her in her grief. He was hardly recognizable as he sat in the dirt with his clothes torn, his head shaven and his body covered in raw and agonizing boils.

But there was something even worse that Job's wife may have considered. In the past God had blessed Job and his wife beyond words. To Job's wife, the terrible implication in their suffering was clear: Despite Job's godly integrity, he and his family had lost Heaven's blessing. God was clearly very angry with Job and her. They had obviously done something that had unleashed the wrath of Heaven. And the result was so bitter that to Job's wife, death was a way of escape from the pain. God, she knew, is the giver and taker of life, and it seemed to her that He was obviously mad at them. Perhaps the intent of Job's wife was that her husband should provoke God further so that death would come quickly.

But Job refused his wife's admonition to curse God, and instead, he worshiped. In speaking of Job's sacrificial worship, Charles Spurgeon said:

> When you are bowed down beneath a heavy burden of sorrow, then take to worshipping the Lord, and especially to that kind of worshipping which lies in adoring God, and in making a full surrender of yourself to the divine will, so that you can say with Job, "Though he slay me, yet will I trust in him." That kind of worshipping which lies in the subduing of the will, the arousing of the affections, the bestirring of the whole mind and heart, and the presentation of oneself unto God over again in solemn consecration, must tend to sweeten sorrow, and to take the sting out of it.[3]

Experts tell us that if we are ever in a building that is on fire and filled with smoke, we shouldn't take even one small breath. The smoke will kill us within minutes. Instead, very quickly, we should drop to our knees and crawl. The air is hot and will cause the smoke to rise, leaving life-giving oxygen close to the ground. That is why in such a fiery environment we should get low, and do it speedily. That's what Job did in his fiery trial—he bowed low before the Lord—and that is what you and I must do when the heat of tribulation suddenly traps us. It's in a low position that we will find life-preserving oxygen.

If you are a Christian, you have the consolation of knowing that you have God's favor in Christ. He is your righteousness, and you must keep in mind that you have the promise that God will work *all* things for your good. Unlike Job, his wife, and the poor mothers of Bethlehem, and unlike millions of others who are blindsided by life, we have amazing consolation in Christ. If you are unsaved, in order to survive your fiery trials, you must repent and put your trust in Jesus Christ.

ONCOMING TRAFFIC

When I first arrived in the United States from my home country of New Zealand back in 1989, I was horrified to see cyclists alongside the roads riding toward oncoming traffic. I had never seen it done before, and I thought it was careless. According to the National Highway Traffic Safety Administration, between the most recent turn of the century and 2009, there were 466,000 bicycle injuries and a massive 7,041 deaths in the United States alone.[4] Taking safety precautions could have prevented many of these deaths.

It makes sense for us to be prepared for tragedy, because we will not avoid its fatal blow if we are hit by it unawares. The way to avoid being crushed by life is to have faith in God to such a point that we can say, as Job would later proclaim, "Though He slay me, yet will I trust Him" (Job 13:15). Have you come to that point? Get there quickly, because the problem that we have in understanding our suffering isn't with God. The Lord is 100 percent trustworthy.

JOB AND KARMA

Job 2:11–7:21

It didn't take long for the news about Job and his wife to spread to Job's friends. When they heard of his adversity, three of his friends came quickly to comfort him. When they arrived, they were horrified by what they saw. Job was in such a sad state that his friends didn't even recognize him. They wept, tore their robes, threw dust on their heads, and sat on the ground with Job for seven days and seven nights. Job's grief was so evident to his friends that they didn't speak a word to him that entire week.

Job finally broke the silence and began to lament the day he had been born. He wished to God that he had never seen the light of day. He was so bitter and full of grief that he wanted to die, saying, "For the thing I greatly feared has come upon me, and what I dreaded has happened to me" (Job 3:25). He had lost his beloved children, his great wealth, his health, his looks, his dignity and the support of his wife. But he still had his friends. He had three faithful friends who had come to comfort him—wonderful friends who had dropped everything to be by his side.

Oliver Wendell Homes said, "Friendship is the breathing rose, with sweets in every fold." Eliphaz the Temanite began the conversation with Job by sweetly complimenting him. He said that Job had instructed many and had strengthened weak hands. Perhaps Job's spirits were slightly lifted by his words. But then Eliphaz shared his true thoughts, and the sweetness faded a bit: "Remember now, who ever perished being innocent? Or where were the upright ever cut off? Even as I have seen, those who plow iniquity and sow trouble reap the same" (Job 4:7-8).

Eliphaz didn't openly say, "Job, you have sinned against God, and He is chastening you," but he inferred it by speaking of the benefits that those who seek and serve God receive. He honored God by singing His praises, saying that the Lord does great things without number: God gives rain to the earth and exalts the lowly; He frustrates the devices of the crafty and catches the wise in their own craftiness (see Job 5:9-16). Eliphaz continued by saying that those who God chastens are happy (see Job 5:17). And this is true. The writer of Hebrews even quotes Eliphaz's words when speaking of God's chastening hand upon His children (see Heb. 12:5). But Eliphaz went on to tell Job that no evil would touch those who seek the Lord. The godly would laugh at destruction and famine, not be afraid of the beasts of the earth and have peace in their tents. They would visit their dwellings and find nothing amiss. Their descendants would be many, and their offspring would be like the grass of the earth. In other words, Eliphaz was saying that to those who are good, God gives good things, and to those who do wrong, God brings hardship. Eliphaz finished his commentary with the firm statement, "Behold, this we have searched out; it is true. Hear it, and know for yourself" (Job 5:27).

But Eliphaz's speech presents some confusion. Job's descendants had been killed; he had no offspring anymore. To Eliphaz, this meant that Job was clearly out of favor with God. Now no doubt God does bless the righteous. And no doubt He does chasten His children when they go astray. But Job maintained that he hadn't done anything wrong, that he'd done nothing to deserve his suffering. So Job first answered Eliphaz with this explanation, and then he directed himself to God. He humbly confessed to the Lord that his words had been rash, but he justified them by speaking of his suffering. He likened his pain to poisonous arrows piercing his very soul and seeping poison into his spirit. Even the tastiest of food turned his stomach. He had nothing for which to live, and he longed for God to take him into the refuge of death. He then said to his friends, "To him who is afflicted, kindness should be shown by his friend" (Job 6:14), and asked, "Did I ever say, 'Bring something to me'? or, 'Offer a bribe for me from your wealth'?" (Job 6:22). He added, "You overwhelm the fatherless, and you undermine your friend. Now therefore, be pleased to look at me; for I would never lie to your face. Yield now, let there be no injustice! Yes, concede, my righteousness still stands" (Job 6:27-29).

So begins the famous contention between Job and his friends. Job's friends maintained that Job's suffering was just in that he clearly must have done something wrong to bring about such disapproval from God in his life. Job said that he hadn't done anything wrong; and we know that Job was in the right, because we have seen behind the veil. We have seen that God Himself had said of him, "Have you considered My servant Job, that there is none like him on the earth, a blameless and upright man, one who fears God and shuns evil?" (Job 1:8). So while it is sometimes true that suffering comes to us by the hand of God to chasten those He loves, that wasn't the case with Job.

The lesson is clear. When a Christian suffers, we must always remember that his or her righteousness in Christ infinitely exceeds the righteousness of Job. When we repent of our sin and put our trust in Jesus, God imputes the righteousness of the Savior to our account. We become morally perfect in the sight of God, because God sees us in Christ—He sees us clothed in the virtue of His Son. So we dare not conclude that when a Christian is suffering, it is because of God's hand of chastening upon that person. When a Christian suffers, we don't know why he or she is suffering, and therefore we should never entertain such thoughts, let alone speak them. The fear of God should keep us from going there. In Luke 13:1-5, Jesus addressed this very subject. Scripture says:

> There were present at that season some who told Him about the Galileans whose blood Pilate had mingled with their sacrifices. And Jesus answered and said to them, "Do you suppose that these Galileans were worse sinners than all other Galileans, because they suffered such things? I tell you, no; but unless you repent you will all likewise

perish. Or those eighteen on whom the tower in Siloam
fell and killed them, do you think that they were worse sinners than all other men who dwelt in Jerusalem? I tell you,
no; but unless you repent you will all likewise perish."

It is human nature to want to solve the problem of suffering
by saying that every tragedy, sickness or accident is some sort of divine retribution. That it is karma. Karma says that suffering comes
to us because we have done something evil either in this life or in
a previous one. Problem solved. But notice how Jesus addressed
suffering. In essence, He said, "So you have concluded that those
who died did so because they did something to deserve such a fate.
But your sins too call for Heaven's wrath. You are still alive only because of God's mercy, so repent and have your sins forgiven before
you are dealt with by justice instead of mercy."

Again, it is natural for most who think about life to want an
explanation for our trials and our grief. Who wants to read a mystery without finding out who committed the crime? This was the
attitude of the disciples in John 9:

Now as Jesus passed by, He saw a man who was blind from
birth. And His disciples asked Him, saying, "Rabbi, who
sinned, this man or his parents, that he was born blind?"
Jesus answered, "Neither this man nor his parents sinned,
but that the works of God should be revealed in him. I
must work the works of Him who sent Me while it is day;
the night is coming when no one can work. As long as I
am in the world, I am the light of the world" (John 9:1-5).

Obviously, thought the disciples, the man had been punished
with blindness, so who was the guilty criminal? Was it the blind
man himself or was it his parents? Jesus said that it was neither.
The man had been born blind so that the works of God could be
revealed in him. And as we read on in the passage, we see that this
was indeed the case. Jesus healed the man of his blindness, and the
man became a witness of the healing power of God.

But that isn't the case for millions who are afflicted with all kinds of diseases. They trudge through life in misery, fighting pain and terrible suffering. They receive no miracle from God, and so we are left with the dilemma as to why God lets them suffer—the "dilemma," that is, if we leave out faith in God. If we follow our natural inclination to want an explanation, then we will end up in a wearisome quandary. But trust looks past the problem and rests in the knowledge that God is faithful and that God knows what He's doing even if we don't—and in most cases, we clearly don't. But this is how it should be: "For as the heavens are higher than the earth, so are My ways higher than your ways, and My thoughts than your thoughts" (Isa. 55:9); "Trust in the LORD with all your heart, and lean not on your own understanding" (Prov. 3:5).

BEING FAITHLESS LEAVES US COMFORTLESS

If Job hadn't had such faith, his terrible suffering would have left him comfortless. He would have had no consolation. Satan had killed Job's children, taken his health and wealth, and stolen his joy in living. The devil had thrown Job into the dirt facedown and had ground his grimy heel into the back of Job's head. But despite his faith in God, Job bemoaned his sad state, saying that his flesh was caked with worms and dust and that his skin was cracked and broken (see Job 7:5)—and he finally began to rail against God. He wasn't going to restrain his sentiments any longer: "I will speak in the anguish of my spirit; I will complain in the bitterness of my soul" (Job 7:11). He looked to the heavens and said:

> Am I a sea, or a sea serpent, that You set a guard over me? When I say, "My bed will comfort me, my couch will ease my complaint," then You scare me with dreams and terrify me with visions, so that my soul chooses strangling and death rather than my body. I loathe my life; I would not live forever. Let me alone, for my days are but a breath (Job 7:12-16).

It's important for us to keep in mind that Job didn't have the insight that we have through the Scriptures. We know it wasn't God who had destroyed Job's life; it was Satan. It wasn't God who had killed Job's children and afflicted him with disease; it was Satan. But Job had no idea what was behind his suffering. In the New Testament, Jesus confirms that the enemy attacks God's children, because He warned us that the devil comes "to steal, and to kill, and to destroy" (John 10:10). The Scriptures further say:

> And behold, there was a woman who had a spirit of infirmity eighteen years, and was bent over and could in no way raise herself up. But when Jesus saw her, He called her to Him and said to her, "Woman, you are loosed from your infirmity." And He laid His hands on her, and immediately she was made straight, and glorified God.
>
> But the ruler of the synagogue answered with indignation, because Jesus had healed on the Sabbath; and he said to the crowd, "There are six days on which men ought to work; therefore come and be healed on them, and not on the Sabbath day."
>
> The Lord then answered him and said, "Hypocrite! Does not each one of you on the Sabbath loose his ox or donkey from the stall, and lead it away to water it? So ought not this woman, being a daughter of Abraham, whom Satan has bound—think of it—for eighteen years, be loosed from this bond on the Sabbath?" (Luke 13:11-16).

When Job was first afflicted, he kept his integrity by saying, "The LORD gave, and the LORD has taken away; blessed be the name of the LORD" (Job 1:21). He understood the sovereignty of his Creator, but now he began to weaken and complain against God.

There are some afflictions in life for which we can't blame anyone but ourselves. These are self-inflicted hardships such as lung cancer caused by a lifetime of smoking, liver or heart disease caused by years of drinking alcohol, problems suffered by those who are gluttons, or sexually transmitted diseases as a result of promiscuity. However, many of our sufferings do come from the enemy, since we are told that the devil walks about as a roaring lion, seeking whom he may devour (see 1 Pet. 5:8) and that our battle isn't against flesh and blood but against spiritual powers (see Eph. 6:12). It may have been those spiritual powers that inspired Job's wife to tell him to curse God and die. That poisonous attitude came from a place Job more than likely least expected it to—his own wife. But that's often how the enemy works. He attacks our most vulnerable position from the place we least expect, just as when Peter, one of Christ's closest disciples, tried to stop Jesus from going to the cross. But Jesus knew the source of Peter's words and said, "Get behind me, Satan!" (Matt. 16:23).

HAVE I SINNED?

In his pre-Scripture ignorance, Job asked four questions in his suffering that we have answers for today. He asked, "Have I sinned? What have I done to You, O watcher of men? Why have You set me as Your target, so that I am a burden to myself? Why then do You not pardon my transgression, and take away my iniquity?" (Job 7:20-21).

It would be wonderful if, in times of trial and pain, this wicked world would ask this first question of Job's: "Have I sinned?" But without a confrontation with the moral law, we human beings have no knowledge of our sinful condition. We think we are good people until the law is applied to our conscience and our conscience is awakened to do its God-given duty.

Job's next question was, "What have I done to You?" The answer to this question, when asked by any one of us, is that we have greatly offended God. We have angered Him by our many sins. When we lie, steal, kill, blaspheme, commit adultery or break any of the Ten Commandments, we sin against God. This is why a guilty King David cried, "Against You, You only, have I sinned, and done this evil in Your sight" (Ps. 51:4).

Job then called God the "watcher of men" and asked his third question: he asked the Lord why he was a "target." This is a big

question in our society today. The answer for Job, and for all sinners, is that the eye of the Lord is in every place beholding the evil
and the good, and each of us is a target for eternal justice. God
personally witnesses our crimes, and His goodness must seek retribution. He witnessed Hitler's atrocities, and He will one day see
that perfect justice in Hitler's life is eventually done. On that day
we will recognize that Hitler didn't get away with anything. God
will see to it that mass murderers are punished. He wouldn't be
good if He allowed anyone who did terrible things to escape justice. He is so good that He will punish rapists, thieves, liars, fornicators, blasphemers, adulterers, homosexuals, pedophiles—in
fact, Jesus warned us that each of us will give an account even for
every idle word we have spoken. That leaves all of us in big trouble on Judgment Day if we haven't repented of our sins. Look at
Scripture's warning:

> But we know that the judgment of God is according to
> truth against those who practice such things. And do
> you think this, O man, you who judge those practicing
> such things, and doing the same, that you will escape the
> judgment of God? Or do you despise the riches of His
> goodness, forbearance, and longsuffering, not knowing
> that the goodness of God leads you to repentance? But
> in accordance with your hardness and your impenitent
> heart you are treasuring up for yourself wrath in the day
> of wrath and revelation of the righteous judgment of
> God, who "will render to each one according to his deeds":
> eternal life to those who by patient continuance in doing
> good seek for glory, honor, and immortality; but to
> those who are self-seeking and do not obey the truth, but
> obey unrighteousness—indignation and wrath, tribula-
> tion and anguish, on every soul of man who does evil, of
> the Jew first and also of the Greek; but glory, honor, and
> peace to everyone who works what is good, to the Jew
> first and also to the Greek. For there is no partiality with
> God (Rom. 2:2-11).

I woke up one morning to once again hear about another all-too-common mass shooting in the United States. This time a man had shown up at a movie theater and shot anyone inside who moved. I predicted, as I had in other such scenarios, that experts would be called in to determine the profile of a killer. They would ask, "What would drive a man to do such a thing to his fellow human beings? Had he been molested as a child? Had he been bullied? Was he a loner who found it hard to make friends? Had he lost his job and found it hard to obtain employment?"

While these are important questions, millions of people experience the issues they address without going out and killing other people. As long as the world rejects the biblical explanation for man's behavior, people will be in darkness as to why normal human beings do evil things.

> Mass killers follow different enough patterns that it's incredibly difficult for researchers to pin down common threads, said Frank Farley, a psychologist at Temple University and the past president of the American Psychological Association. . . . "Even when you pull the pieces together, they really don't add up," said Mary Muscari, a forensic nurse at Binghamton University in New York who has researched mass killers. The histories of mass shooters sometimes show common threads, such as a series of disappointments leading up to the event, Muscari said. But in the end, the spark that drives people to violence is unknown, and the events are rare enough that it's hard to generalize from case to case.[1]

The day before this mass shooting, I had eaten lunch with a pastor who had been saved while he was in prison. When he had first been sentenced to three years in jail, he was so depressed about it that he had been placed in a suicide cell with five other men. He shared with me how he had been awakened in the middle of the night that first night to see one of the other prisoners hanging by his neck in the cell. But rather than attempting to save his life, his fellow inmates urged him on, saying, "Go, go, go—you can do it!" As my friend related this incident, I was horrified at such wickedness. It reminded me of another incident in which I had heard of crowds calling to a suicidal man who stood on a ledge on a high building, "Jump! Do it!"

We don't fully see the depth of wickedness in the human heart because of the restraint brought about by the fear of God and also of criminal law. I have asked people if they would kill for $10,000, and while most say that they wouldn't, some say that they would. When I questioned those who said they would refuse to kill, their response usually came back to their belief in God and the consequent fear of being morally responsible for murder. However, any real fear of God is slowly dissipating from our nation. I would dare to say that many of those who love violent video games and movies would like to know what it feels like to kill another human being, but they carry out their fantasy only onscreen because of their fear of retribution from civil law. But we are even seeing the power of civil law dissipate. When the biblical premise of man being evil by nature is forsaken, society begins to believe that a criminal isn't really responsible for his crimes. People believe instead that societal conditions and life's circumstances are responsible, so the criminal gets a slap on the hand for violent crime since evil is no longer called evil. The lawbreaker is deemed rather to be sick or insane, and he receives rehabilitative treatment rather than punishment.

Just after the mass shooting in the movie theater, *TIME* magazine reported:

> [It's] a mistake to view mass murderers as incomprehensible freaks of nature. For example, we know that the young men who go on murderous rampages are not always sociopathic monsters but, rather, sometimes more or less "regular" men who suffered from crushing depression and suicidal ideation. No reasonable person can imagine how despair could possibly lead to premeditated mass homicide. However, the fact that depression is so frequently accompanied by violent rage in young men—a rage usually,

but not solely, directed at themselves—is something we need to acknowledge and understand.[2]

But if the theater mass murderer was depressed and had rage against himself, it should follow that he would have shot *himself* rather than destroy the precious lives of innocent people. The only thing we need to acknowledge and understand is that homicide is evil and that those who perpetrate such wickedness should face swift justice.

Can you imagine how wicked society would be if the fear of God and the fear of civil law were completely removed? Imagine how our culture would be if a man could rape and murder with no concern about being punished in the slightest. A scenario like that would reveal to everyone the true heart of humanity.

If we get rid of moral restraint by teaching that we are primates and that there is no God who requires accountability, we *will* get our Eric Harrises and our Dylan Klebolds and our Jeffery Dahmers, and we will get our Columbines, our Virginia Techs and our Aurora, Colorados.

We finally come to Job's fourth question: "Why then do You not pardon my transgression, and take away my iniquity?" (Job 7:21). When Job asked God this question, little did he know how 1,000 years later God would graciously deal with his and our transgressions. God Himself would be manifest in human form and would suffer and die for the sin of the world. Because of that, God would be able to legally, once and for all, pardon our crimes and allow us to live.

CLASS WARS

Our sufferings have nothing to do with karma. They have everything to do with the fact that we live in a world of fallen humanity who chooses rebellion against God over His justice and mercy.

Back in 1978, just one year after movie mogul George Lucas released the first *Star Wars* movie, he built his production company far away from Hollywood, just north of the city of San Francisco.

A number of years later, he decided to expand his studios, but his intentions upset the well-to-do residents in the liberal and wealthy wine-and-cheese county. As his project was heading toward approval with the local authorities, a group of snobbish local residents formed a homeowners' association and sent a letter to Mr. Lucas encouraging him to find a "far more appropriate location for the development." They maintained that his studio would "pose a serious and alarming threat to the nature of [their] valley and [their] community, . . . dwarf the average Costco warehouse" and generate light pollution so that their "dark starry skies would be destroyed." They then hired an environmental consultant and a lawyer, and they began proceedings to stop Lucas's project from going ahead. Lucas's company feared a possible lawsuit by the residents that would delay construction indefinitely, so he sold the land to a development company—for low-cost housing.[3]

Such is the way of God with this sinful world. If we don't want Him in control, He will give us our heart's selfish desire—and He will give us the regret that comes with it.

JOB AND JUSTICE

Job 8:1–9:35

The words of Job's comforters were mingled with truth. His friends were there to comfort and encourage him. However, their belief that Job was suffering for his sins soon became very clear. In Job 8 Bildad the Shuhite told Job that his words were like wind—that they had no substance. He insisted that the Almighty didn't pervert justice. And despite the fact that Job regularly made sacrificial offerings for his beloved children, Bildad frankly told his friend that God had judged his children and killed them for their rebellion (see Job 8:2-4). He told Job that if he were pure, God would be prospering him:

> If you were pure and upright, surely now He would awake for you, and prosper your rightful dwelling place. Though your beginning was small, yet your latter end would increase abundantly (Job 8:6-7).

Bildad was right—God doesn't pervert justice. Job knew that his children were sinners, and he feared that they may have cursed God in their hearts, so he didn't disagree with what he heard from Bildad and the others. After all, these were his friends. So after listening to Bildad present these uncontestable facts, Job asked the most profound of questions: "But how can a man be righteous before God?" (Job 9:2).

Job's question begs another question: What does it mean to be righteous? One person's perception of the word differs from another. The key to the answer is in the question itself. Job didn't ask, "How can a man be righteous *before man*?" If we sought to be righteous before other people, all we would need to do is show outward piety. Giving to the poor, feeding the hungry, helping others and offering kind words are all we would need to be declared extremely righteous by man. However, to be righteous *in the sight of a holy God* means to be morally perfect in thought, word and deed, and the only way to determine whether or not we come up to that standard is to look to God's perfect Law: the Ten Commandments.

THE STANDARD

I have talked to many people about how we as human beings can be righteous before God. I have learned that when confronted by the Ten Commandments, we either ask how we can be made right with God, or we try to justify, or excuse, ourselves. If we try to justify ourselves, we normally do that in one of three ways:

1. We trivialize the nature of our sins ("My lies were *white*," "The things I stole were small," etc.).
2. We say that the wrong we did was in the past.
3. We insist that our good deeds outweigh our bad ones.

Each of these attempts to declare that we are innocent has obvious flaws. As human beings, we may trivialize sin, but God doesn't. He is perfect and utterly holy. A lie is a lie, no matter how we may color it, and the Scriptures warn, "Lying lips are an abomination to the LORD" (Prov. 12:22). Now we may not understand what it means to be utterly holy, but we can get a glimpse of the standard of a judge by the sentence he hands down for a crime. For example, God warns us that all liars will have their part in the lake of fire (see Rev. 21:8). The crime of lying is extremely serious in God's eyes.

Trivializing Our Sins

I once took a man who was in his mid-20s publicly through the Ten Commandments. As many people do, this young man trivialized his sins. He said that his lies were only white lies that he had told in the past. He admitted to stealing, but he said that it had happened when he was just a kid. His inference was that a young child doesn't know right from wrong. When I asked what it was that he had stolen, he answered, "I just took a pen from work." I laughed and said, "So you were a *working* kid?" The crowd also laughed, and that's when he realized that he couldn't wriggle his way out of this lie. He admitted that he had been 18 years old when he had stolen the pen. It's been said that taking the easy path is what makes men and rivers crooked. Lying may create an easy path through life for some, but that ease will stop on Judgment Day.

Saying Our Wrong Was in the Past
When we attempt to justify our guilt by saying that what we have done was done in the past, we forget that *everything* we do is in the past. We reason that our sin was so far in the past that it should be forgotten by God, or that we did those things when we were young and didn't understand right from wrong, and now that we have matured, we don't do those wrong things anymore. But we are mistaken in these assumptions.

In 2012 a Nazi named Laszlo Csatary—accused of complicity in the killings of 15,700 Jews during World War II—was found to be hiding in Budapest, the capital of Hungary:

> The Simon Wiesenthal Center announced today that its chief Nazi-hunter, Israel director Dr. Efraim Zuroff, last week submitted new evidence to the prosecutor in Budapest regarding crimes committed during World War II by its No. 1 Most Wanted suspect Laszlo Csatary. . . . The evidence submitted by Zuroff to Prosecutor Dr. Gabor Hetenyi related to Csatary's key role in the deportation of approximately 300 Jews from Kosice to Kamenetz-Podolsk, Ukraine, where almost all were murdered in the summer of 1941. . . . According to Zuroff, "This new evidence strengthens the already very strong case against Csatary and reinforces our insistence that he be held accountable

for his crimes. The passage of time in no way diminishes his guilt and old age should not afford protection for Holocaust perpetrators."[1]

During World War II, Csatary had served as a senior Hungarian police officer in what is now the Slovakian city of Kosice but which was then under Hungarian rule. He was complicit in the deportations of thousands of Jews from Kosice and its environs to the Auschwitz death camp in the spring of 1944. Csatary treated the Jews in the ghetto of Kosice with cruelty, whipping women and forcing them to dig holes with their bare hands. In 1948 a Czech court condemned him to death after a trial held in his absence. Csatary fled to Canada and worked as an art dealer, using a false identity, before being unmasked in 1995 and forced to flee the country. The fact that his crimes were in the past was irrelevant.

Believing Our Good Deeds Outweigh Our Bad Ones

The third straw people grasp at to justify sin is to say that our good deeds outweigh our bad deeds. This is the basis for most religions outside Christianity. People who believe this way acknowledge their sins, but they insist that if we utter enough prayers, suffer enough pain lying on a bed of nails or sitting on a hard pew, give enough to the poor, repent enough of our sins, confess enough to a priest, do enough good works, then our good deeds will outweigh our bad ones. But the fallacy of such a view is shattered in a moment by comparing it to criminal law: "Judge, I raped and murdered that woman, but I would like you to take into account that I gave money to the Red Cross last year and that I'm also involved in a service group that helps the community." What sort of sick individual could think that a judge would take into account these good works in light of a heinous crime? An attempt to excuse or justify oneself in this way would indicate that the criminal didn't consider his crime of rape and murder to be very serious. A good judge would throw the book at such a slow-witted and callous individual.

Perhaps you are thinking, *But that's an earthly courtroom. We are talking about God. He's all-loving and kind.* Do you really think that an earthly judge has a greater sense of justice than God does? When Bildad asked, "Does God subvert judgment? Or does the Almighty pervert justice?" it was rhetorical. The question doesn't need an answer. God is *infinitely* more just than any earthly judge. He will not subvert or pervert justice in the slightest.

You say, "But rape and murder are a little different from lying and stealing and looking at someone with lust." They *are* different, but that doesn't negate their seriousness in God's eyes. In the Lord's pure eyes, our sins are worthy of the death sentence and damnation.

GOD ISN'T ABSENT FROM OUR LIVES

But Job knew that he could never justify his sin or the sin of his children. He still recognized, even in his terrible grief, that God knew what He was doing. Despite his sorrow, Job began to speak of God's wisdom and greatness. He said, "He removes the mountains, and they do not know when He overturns them in His anger; He shakes the earth out of its place, and its pillars tremble; He commands the sun, and it does not rise; He seals off the stars" (Job 9:5-7).

Before I became a Christian, God to me seemed a distant heavenly figure who had little or no part in earthly affairs. However, the moment I was converted, I began to understand that the sun rises because God *causes* it to rise. He spoke the sun into existence and set it in motion so that its rays would hit the earth, and He guides every one of the trillions upon trillions of light beams that race at the speed of light to ripen apples and tomatoes. Nothing happens without God's permissive hand. Without God, volcanoes don't erupt, the earth doesn't quake, the sun doesn't rise, the stars don't shine, the heavens don't exist, dogs don't bark, apples don't grow, and seeds aren't sown. The Lord holds our very breath in His hands. In Him we live and move and have our being (see Acts 17:28). As water saturates the oceans, His presence saturates life:

Great is our Lord, and mighty in power; His understanding is infinite. The LORD lifts up the humble; He casts the wicked down to the ground.

Sing to the LORD with thanksgiving; sing praises on the harp to our God, who covers the heavens with clouds, who prepares rain for the earth, who makes grass to grow on the mountains. He gives to the beast its food, and to the young ravens that cry (Ps. 147:5-9).

Even when life makes no sense to us, we can rest in the knowledge that it makes sense to God. If He is involved in every detail of the universe, then He is surely aware of our pain! Things may look bad to us, but God is working toward something good in the midst of our worst situations.

GROWING OLD DISGRACEFULLY

Although Job acknowledged God's wisdom and greatness, in his discouragement over his painful circumstances, he lamented the fact that the life he knew was quickly draining from him. He said, "Now my days are swifter than a runner; they flee away, they see no good. They pass by like swift ships, like an eagle swooping on its prey" (Job 9:25-26).

Our life is truly like a fog that appears for a moment and then vanishes away. It seems as if it were only yesterday that I met my beloved wife and was married. Then we had kids. Our children quickly grew up, got married and showed up on our doorstep with offspring of their own.

Being a grandparent wasn't a status that I slipped into easily. It may have had something to do with the way my daughter introduced me to my first grandchild. She dropped into our home with her newborn baby, pointed her toward me, smiled and said, "There's Gramps." *Gramps!* In a moment I felt dragged from my youth to a convalescent home, and I didn't like it. From that day I fought the "grandfather" word. I encouraged my posterity to call me Super-dad. That didn't work. I tried Forefather and a few other words, but I finally reluctantly ended up accepting Grandpa.

At present I have nine grandchildren and more in Heaven because of tragic miscarriages. Soon my beautiful grandchildren will have children of their own, and, God-willing, they will bring them to our home to meet Methuselah-pa. As each day passes faster than a speeding train, I know that I may be with the Lord by the time you are reading this book. Death is a fact of life that we can't escape, but we can know that it has lost its terrible sting through our trust in Jesus and our steadfast hope of salvation.

When Sin Hits the Fan

But Job did not have this good news. He not only lamented that his days were passing quickly, but he also cried out that there was no mediator to plead his case before God:

> For He is not a man, as I am, that I may answer Him, and that we should go to court together. Nor is there any mediator between us, who may lay his hand on us both (Job 9:32-33).

Job didn't have the Law to show him that his sin was "exceedingly sinful" (Rom. 7:13). Like most unregenerate men, he had no idea as to the depths of depravity in his own heart. But if he *had* been able to catch a glimpse of his sin and his personal guilt, he would never have wanted to go to court with His Creator.

Job didn't realize it, but sin had soaked him through and through. No doubt he knew that he was a sinner; but without the Law, he didn't understand the depth of his sins. The Law shows us that we are sinking in an ocean of evil. Paul said, "I know that in me (that is, in my flesh) nothing good dwells" (Rom. 7:18). He spoke of sin being "exceedingly sinful" (Rom. 7:13). We are born with a sinful nature, and it permeates our very being, justly destining the best of us to the terrors of a very real Hell.

One day when Sue, my wife, wasn't well, I decided to get a blender so that I could make her smoothies. I purchased the blender, and Sue and I both stood at the kitchen counter and fed blueberries, water, ice and honey into the machine. A few seconds later, there it was: a cool, blue, delicious smoothie. I took the lid off the blender and reached across the counter to grab Sue's glass. It was then that my hand hit the switch on the blender and sent smoothie all over Sue's blouse, into my hair and onto the kitchen ceiling. I was able to get the stain off the ceiling and out of my hair, but we had to throw Sue's blouse away, because we couldn't remove the stain in it.

When King David gave himself to secret sin and then found out that Bathsheba had become pregnant, he thought he could easily smooth things over (see 2 Sam. 11-12). He couldn't. Instead, his sin hit the fan and caused massive repercussions. No matter how delightful sin may taste, it stains horribly and brings with it tragedy beyond words.

SELF-DEFENSE

It has been said that he who goes to court and defends himself has a fool for a client. Many a person is in prison because he thought that he could make a good case for himself when he could not. None of us can justify ourselves before a holy God who has seen our secret sins from His own perspective of unqualified holiness. Each of us needs a good lawyer, someone who will plead our case.

One day I received a call from my daughter. I could tell that she was distressed about something by the tone of her voice. Her children had been staying at our house, and one of my grandkids had dropped my iPad and cracked it. The iPad still worked okay, but Rachel insisted that she buy me a new one. I told her that a cracked iPad wasn't a problem, and I told her to tell the guilty child that all was well. I then rushed out and purchased a new one, and within the hour I was telling my grandson that he could keep my old iPad. I defended my grandson, and then I paid for the damage his actions had caused. The moment he heard the good news, my grandson's sorrow turned to joy. I told him that every time he looked at the broken iPad, he was to remember how much I loved him.

My sorrow turned to joy too the moment I understood that God made all things right for humankind through the cross. I am forever mindful of God's love for me when I consider how I had seriously broken His perfect Law. Job's lament, as we saw earlier, was, "Nor is there any mediator between us, who may lay his hand on us both" (Job 9:33). But God in His kindness provided humanity with one. As Christians, we have a counsel for our defense—an advocate who stands in the presence of God and pleads our case. Look at what the Scriptures say about Jesus Christ: "For there is one God and one Mediator between God and men, the man Christ Jesus" (1 Tim. 2:5).

Here is 1 John 2:1 from the *Amplified Bible*:

> My little children, I write you these things so that you may not violate God's law and sin. But if anyone should sin, we have an Advocate (One Who will intercede for us) with the Father—[it is] Jesus Christ [the all] righteous [upright, just, Who conforms to the Father's will in every purpose, thought, and action].

One of the most common accusations against Christians is that we are weak people who need a crutch in life. Yet while many people refuse the "crutch" of the gospel, they lean on other things to get them through their challenging times without God's help. When a Job experience hits them, some lean on friends and make it through. Others soak themselves in alcohol. Some give themselves to drug abuse or clutch cigarettes in order to cope with daily trials. They make it through life's trials. But they make it *through* to what? What is the destination of those who live without God? This life may have many pleasures that help us to get by, but these pleasures are only temporal. Regardless of what pleasure we put our hand to, it doesn't last. This was the theme of Solomon's philosophy in Ecclesiastes. He spoke of the futility of life because of the reality of impending death.

Even though Job didn't know the gospel story, and even though he grieved in his sorrow, he clung to the fact that God was good and wise. And God was. He allowed Job to experience terrible pain, but He knew that in the end Job was going to be okay.

It is the same for us. God provided us with a Savior not to give us a smooth flight without trials but to give us a safe landing. Jesus was given to us to save us from *future* wrath (see 1 Thess. 1:10). A parachute is for the jump, not for the flight, and as we sit on this flight we call life, the turbulence makes the Christian long for the jump. We don't want to leave our precious loved ones or to suffer with some terrible terminal disease, but for those who are born again, the serpent of death has lost its venom.

5

JOB AND TOUGH QUESTIONS

Job 10:1-7

Animals, as I am sure you know, are different from human beings. They don't have the ability to talk as we do. Neither do they seem to appreciate color, beauty, music or humor. A dog may wag its tail at my antics, but I will wait a long time before I see it crack a smile or burst into laughter. Believe me, I have tried to produce this result. I have looked into the eyes of my mutt and said, "If you would just say something—just one sentence—or burst into laughter, you would make us both billionaires overnight." But my dog has just looked at me as though I was some sort of nut.

The point is, animals do not understand the deeper things of life. They live in the here and now, completely unaware of their origin and totally unconcerned about their future. The sad thing is that many people are like them. Instead of looking to God to find out what He has to say about the hard-to-understand matters of life, these people live only in the immediate and try to come up with their own explanations for life's difficulties.

As Job continued his dialogue with his friends, he cried out to God again in his sorrow and pain, this time with a knotty question. He prayed, "Do not condemn me; show me why You contend with me. Does it seem good to You that You should oppress, that You should despise the work of Your hands, and smile on the counsel of the wicked?" (Job 10:2-3).

RAY COMFORT

Job had lived in the fear of the Lord, resisting the temptations to sin—yet God had brought all this suffering upon him and at the same time seemed to be *smiling* at the counsel of the wicked. *It didn't make sense.* Didn't God see what was happening? Job, a good man, was suffering, while the world was filled with evil men who were flourishing. Did God punish the good and bless the evil?

We will look more particularly at that question in chapter 11 of this book, but the concern now is, where do we turn with tough questions like this one? Do we look to the Lord, or to our own reasoning? Job asked the Lord, "Do You have eyes of flesh? Or do You see as man sees?" (Job 10:4). The answer to Job's question is the answer to our sticky situations. God does *not* have eyes of flesh, and He does *not* see as man sees. The biblical references to God's "eyes" are examples of what we call anthropomorphism. This is the attribution of a human behavior or of human characteristics to God. We say that God has ears and eyes simply so that we can relate to the fact that He hears and sees. But our brains are never as dull as when we think about what God must be like, and our words are never so lacking as when we try to explain the eternality and power of our Creator.

Think about God's mind for a moment. He knows *everything*. All knowledge is His. There is nothing that God does not know. In our small minds we may think this means that God can answer any question, that His IQ is phenomenal. But that is not what is meant by God having all knowledge. Resident in the infinite mind of God is knowledge of you as a person. He knows you by name. He knows how many hairs are on your head. He sees the multitudes of your thoughts as they continually pass through your mind. Think about it: God has seen every impression, every dream, every daydream, every nightmare, every imagination, every judgment and every contemplation that you have ever conjured up in your cranium from the moment that your mind was set in motion. The Lord sees the core of every bone in your body, every drop of blood running through the myriad veins that weave their way through your complex frame. Your Maker has heard every beat of your pounding heart from the moment of your conception in the womb of your mother. God sees every single atom that makes up your amazing body, because He created each individual particle. If we multiply that knowledge by the billions of people who have been created and have died since the beginning of time, we get an extremely minuscule glimpse of the infinitude of the mind of Almighty God.

But for millions of individuals, the thought that God has a mind and that He minds what we do hardly enters their minds.

The infinite mind of God conceived the universe and brought it into being by speaking it into existence. Atheists, however, reject this fact. They have no idea where or how life began. They theorize that there was an explosion of nothing that created everything. But it would be infinitely easier to believe that all songs came to exist without a songwriter—that Paul McCartney's melodic "Yesterday," John Philip Sousa's "The Stars and Stripes Forever" and Beethoven's Fifth Symphony all composed themselves from nothing. The atheist argues against such thoughts by saying, "But music isn't living. Life brought itself into being because it is alive, and it has that ability." But all life randomly coming from non-life—an explosion of lifeless rocks giving life to life—is scientifically impossible.

In a video produced by *TIME* magazine called *Life in the Universe: Easy or Hard?* a respected scientist said that it was fortunate that intelligent life randomly happened for our lone planet. He explains:

> Paul Davies, the Cosmologist at Arizona State University and the author of the book *The Eerie Silence*, believes that life is statistically just unlikely outside of earth. Life is too complex. Earthlike planets are too rare and no matter how many stars there are in the Universe; when you crunch the numbers—we're probably alone.[1]

"No matter how many stars there are in the universe." *Discover* magazine said, "A study by Yale astronomer Pieter van Dokkum just took the estimated number of stars in the universe—100,000,000,000,000,000,000,000, or 100 sextillion—and tripled it."[2] Dokkum's paper said:

Elliptical galaxies are some of the largest galaxies in the universe. The largest of these galaxies were thought to hold more than 1 trillion stars (compared with the 400 billion stars in our Milky Way). The new finding suggests there may be five to 10 times as many stars inside elliptical galaxies than previously thought, which would triple the total number of known stars in the universe, researchers said.[3]

In other words, these articles are saying that even with the innumerable number of stars out there, there's no way that "chance" could create another earth like ours. But why couldn't it, if it randomly created this earth? *Because it is ludicrous, that's why.* Beauty and harmony cannot order itself out of utter chaos. But for some reason, atheistic evolution believes otherwise in regard to our own earth, even as they do not believe it could happen again. It believes that the beauty and harmony that exist in our universe came out of *nothing*. This kind of convoluted thinking comes from a refusal to acknowledge the mind of Christ, which is the source of all the beauty and intricacy that we see around us.

Albert Einstein said:

In view of such harmony in the cosmos which I, with my limited human mind, am able to recognize, there are yet people who say there is no God. But what makes me really angry is that they quote me for support for such views.[4]

Dokkum puts forth an even more ludicrous view, in the name of science, than the one that says order was created from chaos. He said:

The reason life began in the oceans on earth is because water is essential to life as we know it and also because water at least on a planet in the "Goldilocks zone" (not too hot, not too cold) can be very warm and amniotic. That's a very nurturing environment for life to evolve. . . . Plenty of people believe in the theory of Panspermia—the idea that incoming asteroids from deep space carried the organic compounds that first seeded the earth. And there are some people who even suggest that earthlings are, in fact, Martians who originated as single-celled organisms on Mars, rode to earth aboard rocks blasted off of Mars and then populated our Planet.

Life, he says, spontaneously produced itself from the nonlife of the not-too-hot and not-too-cold ocean. But to have an ocean, there must also be an earth, along with gravity and presumably air to sustain life when it came out of the water. What does he have to say about how these things came to be?

Water is not a simple substance. It is a chemical with the formula H_2O. A water molecule contains three atoms: one oxygen and two hydrogen, each of them connected by covalent bonds. Oxygen is an odorless gas, having the molecular formula O_2, and the two oxygen atoms in it are chemically bonded to each other with a spin triplet electron configuration. Hydrogen, the lightest element in water, in its monatomic form (H1) is the most abundant chemical substance in the cosmos, constituting roughly 75 percent of the universe's baryonic mass. Oxygen and hydrogen are incredibly complex. If you think they are simple in structure, try making some—from nothing. Water is a combination of these two elements. Why did these two elements bond? And why did they bond and make themselves into a gigantic pond that we call the ocean and become "a very nurturing environment for life to evolve"? Did all this water come from nothing? If Dokkum believes that, he certainly is in the Cinderella zone—without a fairy godmother.

Dokkum puts forward another theory. In the quote we just saw, he says, "Plenty of people believe in the theory of Panspermia—the idea that incoming asteroids from deep space carried the organic compounds that first seeded the earth." Huge rocks with life on them came to earth. Who or what created these rocks? What were these extremely complex life seeds made up of (there is no such thing as a simple life form), how did they get onto these massive rocks, and how were they able to survive in the incredible heat that was generated from the big bang that sent them hurtling toward the earth in the first place?

But the insanity evolves. The learned scientist puts forward the idea that we are repatriated Martians: "Earthlings are, in fact, Martians who originated as single-celled organisms on Mars, rode to earth aboard rocks blasted off of Mars and then populated our Planet." Bottom line: When human beings reason without taking into account the mind of God, the result is lunacy. All this to get as far away as possible from "In the beginning God created the heavens and the earth," since it has connotations of moral responsibility.

BEYOND HUMAN UNDERSTANDING

Job had another question for the Lord about the difference between God and man: "Are Your days like the days of a mortal man?" (Job 10:5).

Take some time out of your busyness to think for a moment about the remarkable dimension of "time." We have to wait for time to pass, but God does not, because He created it. God flicks though the width of time as you and I flick through the pages of antiquity in a library. The Scriptures use anthropomorphism by saying that a day to the Lord is like a thousand years are to us. In other words, God is not bound by the dimensions that He has created. This can be seen in the study of biblical prophecy, something we will look at in depth later in this book. God knows the future. He sees through time. Such thoughts are interminably beyond human understanding. God's ability to see is as far beyond our own as His mind is beyond our reasoning.

Arguably, the biggest difference between people and animals is that animals have no sense of justice or truth. They have no understanding of wrongdoing or of its consequences on the future. A dog may bury a bone for later, but it is not interested in the future as we are. Animals don't seem to know that they will someday die, and so they are not potential converts who might be interested in eternal salvation. Mankind, however, is *very* interested in the future. That is why billions of human beings are personally interested in religion. The spiritual consumes our lives. This is because we know that God is eternal and we are not. Each of us is sinking into death, and God is the only known lifeboat.

Sadly, though, just as there are many people who try to reason without the mind of God when it comes to our origins, there are many who do the same regarding the hereafter. Some of them, like dumb dogs, are not even interested in eternity—all they think about is the here and now. It is as if they are in a burning desert with a limited supply of water, but they are so shallow in their reasoning that they do not think to search for more to drink.

Others *are* interested in the hereafter, but they pursue it according to their own reasoning. Hindus practice their religion in the hopes of reaching this eternality of God and of escaping death. So do Muslims, Buddhists and the people of a thousand other smaller religions and sects who hope to somehow get to God and find the precious prize of immortality. These people seek after some kind of spiritual existence because God's "days," to answer Job's question, are *not* like those of mortal man. God's days are eternal, and that is impressed upon the heart of humankind.

If we study these religions, we will find that most of them preach that immorality leads away from immortality. This is because people of any and all belief systems have an intuitive consciousness of human sinfulness and of the fact that God requires righteousness of us. They know that humanity must somehow make the leap from wickedness to righteousness.

But God's moral Law shows us that people are unable to make that leap. When we are ignorant of this fact, the best of us are like an overly ambitious little boy who thinks he can ride his tricycle fast enough to leap from one side of the Grand Canyon to the other. A kind father would take the time to explain to the child about the width of the Grand Canyon. God in His kindness has done that for us by revealing His mind to us in the Law. He showed us that the chasm we are trying to leap—from death to immortality, from sin to righteousness—is an infinite distance. It cannot be done. It is impossible. The only way it could happen is if God Himself built a bridge—and the message of the gospel tells us that this is exactly what He did.

Job had no idea why God would allow the righteous to suffer and seem to smile on the wicked. But God could see things that Job could not. Job could trust Him, and so can we.

JOB, THE HAND-MADE MAN

Job 10:8

Job had spoken of God's ability to see and of God's "days," and now he spoke of the Lord's remarkable ability to create: "Your hands have made me and fashioned me, an intricate unity" (Job 10:8).

There are some who question the existence of God, and yet one of the greatest proofs of God's genius is staring at them in the mirror each morning. Our bodies may not be a pretty sight at that time of the day, but a lot has gone on behind the scenes to make us what we are.

How does this connect to the problem of our suffering? Profoundly! The fact that God designed us in intricate detail tells us several things about Him: He is intricately acquainted with everything about us. He knows how our bodies and our minds work, and He knows exactly what we need to survive and thrive. If God created our bodies so elaborately and amazingly, He clearly cares for us and has a purpose in making us. This is one more proof that we can trust Him.

So let's take a look at these bodies of ours! Imagine that you are looking into the morning mirror. Starting at the top of your body, look first at your hair. Over the next few moments we will work our way down this body of yours that God so intricately created.

Hair is amazing stuff. It grows from follicles within the skin. Inside the follicle is the hair root, and at its base is a bulb. This is where nutrients are received and new cells are formed to grow the hair. Also within the follicle is the dermal papilla, where nutrient-carrying blood feeds the hair bulb. Anchored in there as well is an oil gland that lubricates the hair and keeps it healthy and shiny along with a tiny muscle that holds everything to the follicle. It is said that hair is stronger than steel, yet it's soft and congenial to the human touch.

Each hair is a living entity, and it grows in a slightly different direction from the rest of the crop, pushing through from the very shallow soil of human flesh. Overall, hair is a bushy plant, sometimes straight, sometimes curly, coming in a variety of attractive colors—from red to brown to blond and black. The great thing about this plant is that it doesn't have to be watered.

We tend to take hair for granted—until it starts to fall out. If that happens and we want a hair transplant (to replant the plant), it will cost us an arm and a leg. This is because there are no fields of hair waiting to be harvested. The process of hair growth is so incredibly complex that the greatest scientists can't grow even one hair independent of the human body. In order to do a hair transplant, surgeons are forced to harvest hair from the back of our heads, and that's painful, both to our bodies and our pocketbooks.

Each of us has between 100,000 and 150,000 hairs on our head. Interestingly, these hairs are made from the same materials that make up fingernails, bird feathers and reptilian scales. Our bodies are covered in an estimated 10 million hair follicles (only the palms of our hands and the soles of our feet have no hair follicles and are thus hairless).[1]

The "soil" from which our crop of hair grows is a fine layer of skin that was historically highly prized by various groups of warring peoples. Skin is very strong, although soft to the touch, and its main function is to keep our insides in. Without the life-giving blood that flows beneath it, skin would be nothing but a piece of hardened leather. But prick it with a sharp pin and out spurts blood like Texas oil. This is because our eight pints are under very controlled pressure, and if our blood pressure gets out of control, we become in danger of a heart attack.

Our heart-pumped blood travels around our body in a mass of tiny vessels that look like a New York City roadmap on steroids. If you want to confuse a person who believes in atheistic evolution, ask him what it was that came first: the blood, the blood vessels, or the heart. If he says that it was the heart, ask him why a heart would evolve when there was no blood to be pumped anywhere. It would have nothing to beat for. If he says that the blood vessels came first, ask him why they would evolve when there was no blood. If he says that the blood evolved first, ask him how it made its way around when there were no blood vessels in which to travel and no heart to pump it. You could also ask him how and when the lungs came into the equation (if you have the heart to keep pressing him), because blood needs to be oxygenated when it flows around the body, or we will die.

The only rational explanation for any of these questions is that the heart, the blood, the blood vessels and the lungs were all created at the same time.

Despite these logical thoughts, many believe that everything developed through a very slow process of evolution. They believe that from nothing the scientifically impossible happened: there was a big bang. The bang left nothing but rocks, and the rocks became human beings, dogs, cats, horses, cows, giraffes, kangaroos, elephants, tigers, sheep and goats. Each of these creatures had a heart, blood, lungs and blood vessels that were held in by skin, and fortunately they came in male and female models, having the ability and the parts to reproduce after their own kind. If you are one of those people who believes that, look back into the mirror, and let's do some more thinking.

THE SELF-MADE MAN

Let's play the evolution game and see if we can win. You are the ingenious force of evolution, and you are figuring out how to evolve the human body. We have already looked at hair and skin, but the whole structure would be a flop without bones, so putting the rest of this body together is going to require some serious thought.

You will need a lot of bones for your theory to hold up—a total of 206. These will need to be living (try breaking one and find out how it feels if you don't believe that bones are living), and they will need to have marrow inside them that will produce blood cells from the food that will come into the body through an opening in the face. The 206 bones will be joined together with sinews, ball-and-socket joints, synovial fluid and ligaments so that the body will be able to walk, bend, twist, turn and chew. The bones will also need to have the ability to grow from infant-sized to adult-sized while keeping their shape and growing in proportion to all the other bones in the body.

Let's go back to the top of the structure. You will need special bones that fit together to encase the brain, the fluid surrounding the brain (designed specifically for impact resistance) and the nerves that connect to the rest of the body, taking messages about how to keep things running smoothly. And then you will have to give deep thought to developing the brain, because the brain is the control center that will make the rest of the body parts work together. Without it, nothing will work as it should. We will talk more about developing the brain and its bone casing in just a moment.

If you believe in the theory of evolution, you no doubt reject everything I'm saying, because you have been taught that evolution doesn't think, that evolution is responsible for the incredible genius of nature but that it has no intelligence. Okay, let's recognize that premise, but let's continue to make believe that you are evolution and that you are making a human body, because I want to make an important point.

SKULLDUGGERY

We have already begun the process of the skull's design. You will need to think ahead when growing the skull, because eyes will need to evolve eventually so that the body will be able to see what it's doing and where it's going. The eyes will come in a variety of neat colors—blue, green, brown or a combination of these. And since you will also need to produce the eyes, you may as well know now that you will need to come up with 137,000,000 light-sensitive cells as well as focusing muscles that will be able to contract 100,000 times a day to keep things in focus. The focusing muscles will not work until they are *fully* evolved, so the eyes will be useless until that time. Then, when the muscles are fully evolved, they will need to be programmed to focus without conscious involvement from the brain. Don't forget to grow a matching pair.

So the skull's casing will need two sets of two holes, or sockets—one set for the eyes (which will need to be lubricated and attached to the head with a mass of muscle and will include two involuntarily blinking devices) and one set for the ears, which are going to evolve in time as well.

The two ears, by the way, will need to be placed at an angle in order to capture sound, and they will need circular labyrinth grooves to send the sound to the brain through an ear hole. For the brain to make sense of what it hears, you will need to develop high-speed connecters that are able to distinguish between the pleasurable strains of good music or the shrill sounds of a screaming baby.

Don't forget that you will also need a hole in the front of the skull for the mouth and another for the nose. The mouth, which you will need to grow, will need to have soft pliable lips and will have to work closely with the tongue, teeth, taste buds and automatic salivary glands that will be needed for lubrication. You will want to make a voice box and a tongue for speech, and these will have to be connected to the completely evolved brain or the body will be left speechless. Make sure also that the tongue and the inside of the mouth have at least 10,000 taste buds that will be able to savor the fuel that will be necessary to keep this body going. And don't forget to implant "desire" into the brain, or there will be no appetite for the fuel.

Keep in mind that you will need to have two sets of matching teeth (on the top and bottom of the mouth) to break down the fuel and to send it downhill to the process department: the stomach. While we are thinking about the stomach, I should mention that this will have to be carefully thought out, because on the trip down, the fuel will come to an intersection leading to two avenues: one that goes toward the lungs and another that leads to the stomach. The lungs, incidentally, are two automated mechanisms that work together to pull in air and to separate the evolved oxygen and then to send it through the evolved blood vessels to keep the flesh alive. So after the fuel is broken down by the two matching sets of living teeth, you will need a traffic cop at the intersection, who will direct the fuel to the stomach and air to the lungs. Mess that one up, and the body will choke to death.

If you are a believer in the theory of evolution, don't you think it's a little strange that after billions of years of evolution, nothing is still evolving? The eyes of 1.4 million kinds of animals, birds, fish and insects are all in sets of two and fully evolved so that they work. There are no half-evolved eyes anywhere in any blind and half-evolved animal. The ears of all creatures are also fully working. So are the teeth, lungs, kidneys, hearts and livers. Legs, feet, toes and reproductive organs are all fully evolved and working well.

Nothing is still evolving, because everything is at the point of being fully functional. Birds have two wings that work. Fish have all necessary sets of gills and fins. It's as though a great Designer made all these things at one time. Atheist Professor Richard Dawkins gets around the little problem of everything being fully evolved by saying that everything just has an *appearance* of design.[2] His followers don't question these thoughts because if they can believe in evolution, they will swallow anything—which brings us to the evolution of the brain.

DON'T FORGET THE MEMORY

You are going to have to create a brain because, as we have mentioned, the brain is the part of the body that makes all the other parts work together. For this you will need to evolve more than 100 billion neurons and a multitude of helper cells, which will nourish and support the neurons that will need to be grown. The brain should be surrounded by protective membranes, and these should be cushioned with fluid-filled hollows called ventricles.

Remember to evolve in the brain a memory bank, a creative zone, an imagination portion and an area for reason. These are to be linked with the spinal cord and the peripheral nervous system. The spinal cord and the nervous system control every part of daily life, from breathing to blinking to memory. Make sure you therefore run nerves from the brain to the face, ears, eyes, nose and spinal cord and then from the spinal cord to the rest of the body. There will be messages coming and going throughout the body, and it's the brain that will make sense of them.

Think deeply, Mr. Evolution, before you make the brain, because there are more complexities involved in this organ. There are three areas in the memory cortex: (1) very short term, (2) short term and (3) long term. Information such as phone numbers (which you only need for half a minute) goes into the short-term area, while the long-term memory will help us in the future to remember things such as the smell of Grandma's baking. These long-term memories can last a lifetime.

You will then need to figure out how to circulate blood through the brain. The blood is what will give the brain its life. Since we are speaking of blood, make sure that it has the ability to coagulate. If that doesn't happen, then the first time there's bleeding in the body, it will lead to certain death, and this whole evolution thing will go nowhere. The way blood will have to clot is extremely complex, so it won't be easy to make blood that can do this by itself. There are two major facets of the clotting mechanism: the platelets and the thrombin system. Platelets are very small and will be made in the bone marrow. These will travel in the blood and wait for any bleeding problems that the body may have. If there is a cut in the skin, immediate chemical reactions will take place, changing the surface of the platelet to make it "sticky." These sticky platelets will then adhere to the wall of the blood vessel at the cut and very quickly form a clot. So the bones that create the blood will need to evolve before the blood, heart and blood vessels do so that they can manufacture the necessary platelets. Keep in mind that the blood won't be able to clot until all these complex factors are in place. This will cause a problem for you, because the body you are making through the millions of years of evolution will keep bleeding to death until all these issues have evolved to maturity.

The brain is infinitely more complex than the most sophisticated computer. Yet it only weighs three pounds, and it is made of meat, so if you tossed it to a dog, the animal would probably eat it without much thought. That idea should make a thinking person think. So give some thought to how you will make the brain before you start making it. If the body you are evolving will be that of an atheist, however, you will probably be able to skip this step.

There's one more important fact for you to keep in mind. You will have to do this evolutionary process for 1.4 million different kinds of animals, birds, fish and insects. Make sure each kind evolves as both male and female and has the ability to reproduce after its own kind—and that will not happen until each one is fully evolved. So you have a few problems to sort out, if you think about it. Thinking is the key.

ATHEIST ATTACK

I wrote a book called *You Can Lead an Atheist to Evidence, but You Can't Make Him Think*.[3] The day the book was published, it bumped Richard Dawkins's book *The God Delusion* off Amazon's number one spot for the "atheism" division. This so angered the atheist community that many of them conspired to bring down the book's ratings by giving it bad reviews. These individuals also advised those participating to make sure they didn't always give the book a one-star rating but to add two stars now and then so that their conspiracy wouldn't be obvious.

Their plan worked. The book began with many five-star ratings from genuine reviews, but once the atheists had written theirs, the average rating went down to two stars, and no one is going to buy a two-star book. I felt frustrated, because I had no recourse. But I thanked God, and then I stood on Romans 8:28: "We know that all things work together for good to those who love God, to those who are the called according to His purpose." So the following email that came to our ministry was very special to me:

I was an atheist for 22 years. Two months ago a Christian friend gave me a copy of Ray's book *You Can Lead an Atheist to Evidence, but You Can't Make Him Think*. God really used this book to open my eyes. I have only one friend who kept trying to reach me. He cared enough about my soul and where I would spend eternity not to give up on me. I would never listen to anyone on the subject of God, and most certainly if you tried to talk to me about it . . . I would end up getting angry.

I was one of those angry skeptics. Great idea to have an atheist foreword the book . . . and he asks, "Are you up for the challenge?" That really grabs your attention! I mocked and ridiculed anyone who believed in God. I called evil good and good evil. Most certainly, "atheism is the epitome of stupidity," like Ray says. I was one of those unreasonable people. The book left me with NO reason for why I didn't believe in God. The reality is true, I didn't want to be morally responsible to God; I loved sin too much, so I denied the existence of God. No other reason.

For the first time, it got me out of my stupidity and shocked me back into reality. I began to fear the "unknown" of what would happen if I died. I began to fear Hell . . . terribly. The truth is, I never thought any further than my nose. I was soundly saved out of atheism! I can say "Praise God!" It is only by His grace that I am even saved today. I put on the Lord Jesus Christ and repented of my wicked, blaspheming ways!

I am thankful to God for His patience! God's patience can only last for so long. I cannot sit by and watch as my family, friends or anyone be sent to Hell. I am so excited to share with others what has happened to me, and I have already been able to share the truth with one of my atheist friends. I am going to give them a copy of Ray's book. I am reading my Bible, and I've visited the church my friend attends.

Thanks, Don

This one was also encouraging:

This is not meant as an insult, but we never imagined writing a letter addressed to you. We have followed Richard Dawkins . . . and, well, you know how he is. We have begun to find "holes" in what Richard Dawkins says and with what we believe. We have been atheists for years, especially my husband. He always would get into arguments with people on the existence of God. If you were to try to pinpoint Daniel on his atheistic views, he would tell you, "I don't need to prove anything. There is no God, just look at all the evil." Then he would sit there with a smug look on his face as if he had just proved his point.

I agreed with almost everything he said. About once a month, there is a group of Christians that goes down to a very busy section of where we live, and they preach. Of course, my husband and a group of his atheist buddies think they always have to go down and "visit." The Christians always greet them with "Hello, friends," and they wave. They could always depend on Daniel and his friends trying to cause trouble. Daniel says he loved every minute of it (I always told him to leave them alone . . . and now he feels bad about it). The Christian guys always tried to get Daniel and his buddies to come talk with them—out in the open.

After months of them asking . . . Daniel decided, with encouragement from his friends, to "prove" his position and debate these Christians! I was down there this time when this whole thing happened! Let's just say, he didn't have a leg to stand on, and he was quite embarrassed. Daniel says that, being the cocky person he was, he really thought he could outsmart these Christians with his "logic."

At one point, he looked back at his buddies, like a call for help, and they just shrugged their shoulders! We always found these Christians fascinating. They never responded hatefully to any of our name-calling. Daniel says, "Oddly enough, they made sense to me . . . but I would never admit that . . . so I just name-called. I made a big mistake trying to debate those nice Christian guys in front of a crowd." His other atheist friends left him surrounded by a bunch of Christians.

The guy Daniel was debating posed one question that changed our whole perspective: "So let me ask you this: you believe nothing created everything?" Daniel was stuck and didn't know what to say. He says, "I tried to make the conversation go my way, but it didn't work. The guy asked me another four times before I finally answered, 'Well, no, not exactly but . . .'" He said, "So you believe something created everything?"

Daniel says he was stuck, he could either (a) leave and make himself look very stupid or (b) pretend to look smart and answer the question. He said, "Yes." Daniel's face turned bright cherry red! He walked over to the Christian guy and whispered quietly, "I guess that makes me more of an agnostic, doesn't it?" Dan (the Christian preacher guy) said, "I was just going to tell you that!" This led into a three-hour conversation with Dan and both Daniel and myself. Dan did what he called the "Good Person Test." We failed. We came to the point of actually believing we would be sent to Hell.

At the end of our conversation, Dan said, "Would you like a Bible?" We were very interested. We took the Bible. He said, "Here, take one of these too" (a *180* DVD and a gospel tract). We took them home and watched the movie. We must say, Ray—very well put and good job on *180*! We can say with absolute certainty (kind of funny, we used to not believe in "absolutes") that we will NOT be listening to or reading anything by Richard Dawkins. In one day, with talking to "preacher-guy Dan" and watching the *180* movie . . . we went from being atheist to agnostic to we don't know what you call us now!

We don't know how much more blind and stupid you can be than we were! We blindly followed Richard Dawkins around, believing everything he said. No more believing "something came from nothing." We were as illogical as they come. We will leave you with this, Mr. Comfort: you make complete sense, unlike us. Hopefully, we are going to talk with Dan again . . . more about God. We never really thought about where we would go if we died, but now we are thinking about it. We agree—we will be sent to Hell, and you would think it should concern us . . . but it still doesn't really.

We've started reading the book of John together, like Dan suggested that we do . . . maybe that will help us understand more. It amazes me how long "preacher-guy Dan" and the rest of his friends kept going down there to preach, even with all the people who acted like my husband and his friends. We're not even really sure why we were atheists.

Thank you for your logic. *180* is good, keep passing it on.

Marrisa and Daniel M.

Job continued to cry out to God for answers in his pain. But in the midst of it all, he recognized that the hand of God had shaped him. In our sorrow we can find comfort in simply recognizing God's greatness, as David also did: "For you created my inmost being; you knit me together in my mother's womb. I praise you because I am fearfully and wonderfully made; your works are wonderful, I know that full well" (Ps. 139:13-14).

JOB AND THE LAW

Job 10:14

A friend once told me about an incident in which his buddy accidentally left his iPad at a pizza restaurant. When the man went back to get it, he found that his tablet had been stolen. Fortunately, he had a tracking application on his iPhone, so he traced the iPad to a seedy part of town. His wife pleaded with him not to go there, but he went anyway.

As he stood outside the pinpointed home, he prayed that God would help him. Just then a police officer pulled up in a car and asked if he needed any help. The man explained about the stolen iPad, and the officer said, "Let's go and get it then."

The door opened to the officer's knock, but after being questioned about the iPad, those inside the home denied any knowledge of its whereabouts. It was then that the iPhone tracked the tablet being snuck out the backdoor of the home. The officer told the homeowner that they had a tracking device, and suddenly the people inside remembered that, ah yes, they did indeed have the iPad.

The eye of God tracks our sin. The Bible says that God's eye is in every place, "keeping watch on the evil and the good" (Prov. 15:3). Job recognized this when he cried out despondently, "If I sin, then You mark me" (Job 10:14**).** Our crimes against the Lord have been trailed by a relentless and perfect Law that will be satisfied with either the payment made on the cross of Calvary or the everlasting damnation of sinners in a terrible place called Hell.

It is because of this that I would like you to take a moment to consider your own moral state before God. Two thousand years ago a man named Nicodemus did this. Nicodemus was a Jewish religious leader who approached Jesus one night with some questions:

> "Rabbi, we know that You are a teacher come from God; for no one can do these signs that You do unless God is with him."
>
> Jesus answered and said to him, "Most assuredly, I say to you, unless one is born again, he cannot see the kingdom of God."
>
> Nicodemus said to Him, "How can a man be born when he is old? Can he enter a second time into his mother's womb and be born?"
>
> Jesus answered, "Most assuredly, I say to you, unless one is born of water and the Spirit, he cannot enter the kingdom of God. That which is born of the flesh is flesh, and that which is born of the Spirit is spirit. Do not marvel that I said to you, 'You must be born again'" (John 3:2-7).

This experience of being born again is the way we find peace with God. Through it God extends His hand of mercy to the guilty sinner.

A Quick Mix

Sometimes when we have a problem, we try to fix it on our own. But this isn't always a good idea.

I'm a CEO. Prestigious though the job may sound, the position comes with some unwanted baggage. This includes board meetings, conference calls, travel and committee meetings. Despite the work they bring, these things are necessities for a ministry as it grows, because they provide a form of checks and balances.

When our ministry was in its infant stages, we worked out of the garage at my house and made decisions without too much thought. If we blew it, it was no big deal, because there were no real repercussions. However, nowadays a wrong decision can have serious consequences for our ministry, so I gladly submit to the counsel of wise men.

One day, however, I decided not to ask for their advice on an issue. There was an alley alongside the entrance of our building that looked like a war zone. It was filled with hundreds of cracks and two really big potholes. Over the years the cracks had become more numerous and the holes had gotten bigger. So I finally told Sue that I was going to secretly buy some quick-drying cement and fill in the holes. I said that I didn't want 400 emails going back and forth saying that the alley would look worse with the holes filled and then a two-hour committee meeting ending with a decision to spend thousands of dollars to have it done professionally after the finances would one day be available.

So early one Saturday morning I snuck around to the hardware store and purchased two heavy packets of quick-drying cement that were designed for roadside potholes. I then grabbed a shovel and set up to do some hard labor.

As I mixed in the water, I was reminded of when as a 13-year-old I had worked on Saturday mornings for a bricklayer so I could save money for my first surfboard. I smiled as I created a small volcano with the cement mix, carefully poured water into the crater and skillfully turned the mixture. There are some things a proficient worker never forgets.

Suddenly the mixture began to get heavy. *This sure is "quick-drying" cement!* I thought. The cement grew heavier and heavier. I realized that I didn't have enough water, and the water source was quite a distance from where I was. I called to Sue, but she didn't hear me. So I quickly ran for more water, filled a bucket and ran back. The mix was getting extremely heavy, and with each turn of the shovel, my back ached terribly.

I hollered for Sue once again to help with extra water, but she couldn't hear me. I dared not leave the hot mix for a second, so I kept turning it the best I could and then tossed some into the first hole. To my dismay, it hardly covered one corner of the smallest hole. It was then that I remembered that concrete mixture shrinks when it's wet. I hit the repair job with the shovel a few times and stood back to look at my workmanship. It looked worse than it had when I had started. So did I. My sneakers and socks were covered in splashes of concrete.

As I drove off, I stopped and looked at the hole and hoped that none of the staff would notice the mess when they arrived at work on Monday. Sue kindly said that she would ask one of the guys to call in the professionals.

"Religion" is man's pathetic efforts to repair the alleyway. All his energies combined are like a man dropping a pound of wet cement into the Grand Canyon, hoping that he can fill it to the top. Through the new birth that Jesus told Nicodemus about, God provided a perfect and smooth road for us. It isn't a repair job. Through this new birth, God makes all things new. Religion paints the building, even though the entire structure is filled with termites. It may look good on the outside, but the inside is eaten through and through. That's what Jesus was telling Nicodemus that dark night 2,000 years ago.

THE DIFFERENCE

There is something that separates Christianity from all the religions of the world: those who are believers in Christ have more than an academic acquaintance with God's Law—they also have a knowledge of the *spiritual* nature of God's Law. Becoming aware of the spirituality of God's Law is what brought me from having only an intellectual and distant knowledge of God to the point of knowing that I needed to be born again. Those who don't have a spiritual knowledge of the Law tend to think of God in terms of human standards. Psalm 50 puts it this way:

> But to the wicked God says: "What right have you to declare My statutes, or take My covenant in your mouth, seeing you hate instruction and cast My words behind you? When you saw a thief, you consented with him, and have been a partaker with adulterers. You give your mouth to

evil, and your tongue frames deceit. You sit and speak against your brother; you slander your own mother's son. These things you have done, and I kept silent; you thought that I was altogether like you" (Ps. 50:16-21).

Notice the references to the seventh and eighth commandments ("You shall not commit adultery" and "You shall not steal," Exod. 20:14,15). Here is someone who "declares" God's statutes and takes His covenant in their mouth, yet they hate instruction. There are many people in this category who have a measure of spirituality but who refuse to heed the warning that Jesus Himself gave (the very One they profess to serve) about the absolute necessity of the new birth (see John 3:1-21). But then in Psalm 50:21 we see the root of their error: they thought that God was just like them—that He didn't make a big deal of sin. They thought that God (like man) was morally tolerant and that He didn't mind things such as theft and adultery.

In 2012, results were published from a study of people's personal beliefs about Heaven and Hell:

Crime rates are higher in countries where more people believe in heaven than in hell, researchers have found. The finding emerged from a study into 26 years of data involving more than 140,000 people from almost 70 nations. The results suggest that people are more likely to feel they can get away with criminal behavior if they don't believe they could be punished in the afterlife. . . . The pair then compared the data to average crime rates in those countries based on homicides, robberies, rapes, kidnappings, assaults, thefts, car crime, drug offences, burglaries and human trafficking. . . . "Belief in hell predicted lower crime rates . . . whereas belief in heaven predicted higher crime rates."[1]

When people believe in a god who has no sense of justice, they give themselves to crime. Those who believe that God will hold us accountable for our actions, however, hold back from wrongdoing for fear of divine retribution. For most the problem is that it is hard to reconcile a God of love with a God who would create Hell. For these people Hell is just for bad people—those in the category of Hitler and other mass murderers.

We see a similar result in another survey: *The Wall Street Journal*, also in 2012, published an article about cheating. University professors had taken 450 participants at the University of California, Los Angeles, formed them into two groups and asked one group to recall the Ten Commandments and the other to recall 10 books that they had read in high school. Among the group who recalled the 10 books, the professors saw typical widespread but moderate cheating. But in the group that was asked to recall the Ten Commandments, they observed no cheating whatsoever.

This happened because God has written "the work of the law" (Rom. 2:15) on the heart of each son and daughter of Adam. We intuitively know that it's wrong to lie, steal, kill and commit adultery. My consolation before I was a Christian was that I had never committed adultery. But my ignorance of the spiritual nature of God's Law gave me the erroneous thought that if Heaven did exist, I would make it there.

Yet Scripture tells us that when we as much as *look* at a woman with lust, we commit adultery in the heart:

> You have heard that it was said to those of old, *"You shall not commit adultery."* But I say to you that whoever looks at a woman to lust for her has already committed adultery with her in his heart (Matt. 5:27-28, emphasis added).

In other words, God's Law doesn't simply require an outward appearance of piety from us. The Law is spiritual; it requires holiness in our thought life (see Rom. 7:14). If you or I hate someone, God considers us to be murderers: "Whoever hates his brother is a murderer, and you know that no murderer has eternal life abiding in him" (1 John 3:15).

C. S. Lewis said this:

Christianity simply does not make sense until you have faced the sort of facts I have been describing. Christianity tells people to repent and promises them forgiveness. It therefore has nothing (as far as I know) to say to people who do not know they have done anything to repent of and who do not feel that they need any forgiveness. It is after you have realized that there is a real Moral Law, and a Power behind the law, and that you have broken that law and put yourself wrong with that Power—it is after all this, and not a moment sooner, that Christianity begins to talk. When you are sick, you will listen to the doctor. When you have realized that our position is nearly desperate you will begin to understand what the Christians are talking about. They offer an explanation of how we got into our present state of both hating goodness and loving it. They offer an explanation of how God can be this Person. They tell you how the demands of this Law, which you and I cannot meet, have been met on our behalf, how God Himself becomes a man to save man from the disapproval of God.[2]

God and the Law are like the sun and its light. We can never separate the two. The moral Law (the Ten Commandments) is the visible and shining light that bursts from God's fiery holy character. The Scriptures tell us that both the Law and God are perfect, holy, just and good. The Law reveals the Lord's likes and dislikes. It is a synopsis of His core attributes. There was no time in eternity when God said, "I wonder what is right and what is wrong . . ." The Law is eternal, and it's universal; it is applicable to the entire human race.

ARE YOU KIDDING?

It is easy for us to be deceived by false advertising. When my family first arrived in the United Sates back in 1989, I could hardly believe that supermarkets were actually *selling* water. It was so weird to me that I took a camera into a store and filmed the bottles of water to show my relatives back in New Zealand. Who would believe that anyone could market and sell common, everyday water that anyone could get from his own kitchen sink? It was like selling sand to desert dwellers.

But you have to hand it to the marketers of bottled water. They told people that tap water was bad, and then they told America that to stay healthy, everyone should drink eight glassfuls of water each day. And America swallowed it. Yet in countries with hot climates where people cannot afford the luxury of daily guzzling gallons of water, people lived just as long. The same is the case in countries such as Russia, where it's too cold to drink vast quantities of water. I have seen friends in America carrying around huge bottles of water because they believe the hype, so I have ribbed them by saying, "Have you heard the latest? Scientists have just discovered that drinking too much water is bad for you. It dilutes the digestive juices and makes the heart work harder, resulting in a greater chance of heart attack." Of course I was only kidding. I too thought that the water was somehow benefiting them. But I have since changed my mind:

> Doggedly following advice to drink at least eight glasses of water a day is said to be of no health benefit to most people and only enriches bottling companies. . . . "We get a lot of fluid from food. Fruit and vegetables are upwards of 90-95 per cent water. Eating an apple a day is a little bit like drinking a glass of water." Australian university lecturer Spero Tsindos, who examines water consumption in the latest edition of the Australian and New Zealand Journal of Public Health, said encouraging people to drink large amounts of water was driven by vested interests. Pricier brands of bottled water can cost more than $3 a litre at New Zealand supermarkets. A Pennsylvania University research review published in 2008 found no evidence that drinking eight glasses of water a day improved skin tone, aided dieting or prevented headaches (except those induced by hangovers).[3]

Our problem is that we are surrounded by clever people whose agenda is to make money at any cost—and it works. These product owners know that human beings are gullible. They can create advertising that makes people feel good about drinking the poison of alcohol. They can make people feel that it is cool to breathe in the smoke of a burning tobacco leaf and slowly kill themselves. They can subtly manipulate us to buy things that we neither want nor need.

Our society wants us to believe that people are basically good and do not really intend any harm. But this is false advertising. And as much as we would like to think that people are good at heart, it is a conviction that many are finding difficult to hold onto. Our prisons are full, and there is corruption in the police force, in politics, on Wall Street and in every area of society. We lock our cars, lock our homes, hold tightly to our wallets and purses in public, and even protect our identity from being stolen. It is actually far easier for us to believe what the Law straightforwardly tells us: man is not good at all—we are born with a sinful nature.

I had an hour-long public clash with a well-known Hollywood psychiatrist who was known as "an expert witness who testifies in high profile trials, and analyzes trials in the media." This woman was horrified that I believed that people are born sinful. She believed that we are fundamentally good and that we go astray because of life's unfortunate circumstances.[4] My convictions, however, don't come from what I see in society. They come from God's Word, and the news media daily fortify that belief with masses of stories of rape, theft, greed, hatred, adultery and murder.

When God gave His commandments to Moses, He was saying, "This is what I am like, and this is what I require." When the commandments are held up as a mirror to sinful humanity, they should send us to the cross of Calvary for cleansing and forgiveness. It was the knowledge of God's holiness and my own sinfulness before Him that brought me to conversion on April 24, 1972, at 1:30 AM.

We will see later on how Job came up against the very same experience.

JOB AND SALVATION

Job 10:14

I knew a man who once looked into having the procedure of hair restoration done. He had heard that more than 100,000 men had received restorations and that the procedure had been so well done that the work was virtually undetectable. As this man debated about whether or not to go ahead with the process, he thought about the fact that if his front tooth fell out, he would have it replaced simply for cosmetic purposes. So he decided to go ahead.

On his fact-finding visit to the surgeon, the doctor didn't bother giving the man a sales pitch. First the doctor gave the man a hand mirror and a comb, and he had him lift up and pull back his hairline so that he could see for himself the bald truth. Then the surgeon showed this man pictures of a client who had once been bald but who now had a mass of healthy hair covering his head. The procedure sold itself.

When we hold up the mirror of God's Law to others and comb through the Ten Commandments with them, we merely show people the naked truth. We do not need to *peddle* the gospel. The Law clearly shows us that we have sinned against God and that we are justly heading for Hell. Job, not knowing God's plan to one day exonerate men and women from our sins, felt despair over his own sinfulness, crying out, "[You] will not acquit me of my iniquity" (10:14). Many people feel that God will not forgive them for things they have done. But the dark fact of Hell, as we saw in the previous chapter, makes the good news of the gospel stand out as a shining lighthouse in the terrible storm of the wrath of almighty God. So what do you see when you look into the mirror of God's Law?

LET'S MAKE SURE

Perhaps you consider yourself to be a spiritual person, and you have been doing the best you can at living your life. You believe in God. You do kind things for others. You confess your sins, but you have never been "born again." As we have already talked about, this is an extremely important matter, because Jesus warned that those who are not born again cannot enter the kingdom of Heaven. So let's make sure that you make it to Heaven, because in light of eternity, nothing else really matters. We have already talked about how a spiritual knowledge of the Law will shed light on a person's spiritual status before God. So let's take a look at the Law of God and let it examine you by putting you on the stand and letting its light expose what you are before the Day of Judgment. This may not be a pleasant experience, but it is a most necessary one. Here we go.

Have you ever lied? Simply answer the question with a yes or a no. Have you stolen anything in your life? Yes or no. Have you ever used God's name in vain, even once? Have you ever looked at someone with lust or hated anyone? If you have done these things, then you are a self-admitted lying thief, blasphemer, murderer or adulterer at heart. So what do you have to say for yourself? How can you justify murder, adultery, lying, stealing and using God's name as a cuss word? Confessing your sins can't help you. That is like standing before a judge and *confessing* that you are guilty as charged. How can that help? Saying that you are sorry and that you will not commit your sin again will not help either. Of course, a criminal *should* be sorry, and of course, he shouldn't commit his crimes again. But what are you going to say to make things right? How can you keep from being guilty on Judgment Day and avoid the damnation of Hell?

We tend to look at sin according to the world's moral standards. We think that lying is wrong because it betrays trust, that stealing is wrong because it destroys society. Homosexual adoption is said to be wrong by many people because children need a mother and a father. If the "morality" of something is based on what works, then it is fine for spouses to lie to each other as long as they find a way to have a relationship that works. Or stealing is morally okay as long as no one notices that he has been ripped off. Or if children raised by homosexuals are proven to be stable and happy, then the lifestyle of homosexuality becomes acceptable. But this perspective is a mistaken one. Rather, sin is wrong for one reason only: God says it's wrong.

All of us have seriously sinned against our Creator; we are under His wrath and we *can't* help ourselves. All we can do is raise our hands in surrender. This is where the new birth comes in.

DEAD MAN'S CURVE

A friend was driving me on a freeway in Los Angeles, and as we exited, I noticed that we were still traveling at a high speed. I quietly said, "I call this next curve 'Dead Man's Curve.'" I didn't need to say any more. My friend immediately applied the brakes.

When it comes to sin, the world applies the accelerator. It drives at breakneck speed toward Hell, but the way to get people to apply the brakes is simply to mention the Ten Commandments. When people look at God's Law with a tender heart, it makes the fact of Hell real to them.

Any Protestant, Catholic or otherwise religious person who is not born again is almost certainly trusting in his own goodness or his own religious works to save him on Judgment Day. People like this are hoping that their praying, fasting, repentance and good works will give them a pass into Heaven. Christians, however, have come to realize that religion cannot save them. They are sinful people who have trusted alone in the person of Jesus Christ for their eternal salvation. This is because the Law has shown them that their good works aren't good, and they suddenly understood that in God's eyes they are criminals and that He is a perfect judge. Therefore, they recognized that anything they offered Him wasn't good at all; it was only an attempt to bribe Him so that He might dismiss their case.

If you are unsaved, you are hopelessly joined to sin and death. No amount of religious wrestling will get you away from it. If you want to live, you have no other choice than to tear yourself away from sin through the acts of repentance and trust in Jesus.

A woman's car broke down late one moonless night in an area with which she was unfamiliar. She was afraid, so she wound the vehicle's windows up tight, locked the doors and turned on the car radio to keep her company. She decided that it would be wise to wait until the morning light before going for help.

A short time later a frantic man appeared at her window and began to yell at her. Frightened, she gestured for him to go away. He left and then returned seconds later with a rock in his hand, smashed the window of her car and pulled her out, much to the woman's horrified protests. As they fell to the ground, a massive train slammed into her car, causing it to burst into flames.

You may consider Christians to be raving lunatics, but all we are frantically trying to do is warn you that you are in terrible danger. The train of God's moral Law is merciless. Your ignorance of the imminent peril won't keep it from coming. Please, soften your heart and listen to the message of the gospel before it is too late.

Fortunately, the Bible tells us that God is "rich in mercy" (Eph. 2:4). Jesus portrayed God as a loving Father who is looking out for the return of His prodigal son. When the father saw his son coming toward him from a distance, he ran to his son, fell upon him and kissed him. You are the prodigal, and God is that father. Think of what the Lord did to save guilty sinners from damnation in Hell: He became a human being and paid our fine so that we could leave the courtroom. That's what took place on that terrible cross 2,000 years ago. The sin of the world fell upon the innocent Lamb of God—He was bruised for *our* iniquities. The sweetest words that any human being will ever hear are the words "Not guilty." Those who are free from guilt on that terrible day will live.

Notice the repetition of the words "only begotten" in the following verses from God's Word:

And the Word was made flesh, and dwelt among us, (and we beheld his glory, the glory as of the only begotten of the Father,) full of grace and truth. . . . No man hath seen God at any time; the only begotten Son, which is in the bosom of the Father, he hath declared him. . . . For God so loved the world, that he gave his only begotten Son, that whosoever believeth in him should not perish, but have everlasting life. . . . He that believeth on him is not condemned: but he that believeth not is condemned already, because he hath not believed in the name of the only begotten Son of God (John 1:14,18; 3:16,18, *KJV*).

The words "only begotten" mean that Jesus was absolutely unique. He was the only One who could pay for the sin of the world, because He was morally perfect, and He was morally perfect because He was God in human form. He proved this by not only suffering for our sins but by resurrecting Himself from the dead:

Therefore My Father loves Me, because I lay down My life that I may take it again. No one takes it from Me, but I lay it down of Myself. I have power to lay it down, and I have power to take it again. This command I have received from My Father (John 10:17-18).

So what are you going to do? Are you going to stay religious, trusting in yourself, or are you going to surrender to the Savior and trust in Him alone so that God can clothe you in the righteousness of Jesus Christ? *Please* surrender, and do it now, because you may not have tomorrow. If you are not sure how to do this, pray a prayer similar to the one King David prayed after his sin was exposed. He had committed adultery and murder, and after his sin was uncovered, he cried:

Have mercy upon me, O God, according to Your loving-kindness; according to the multitude of Your tender mercies, blot out my transgressions. Wash me thoroughly from my iniquity, and cleanse me from my sin.

For I acknowledge my transgressions, and my sin is always before me. Against You, You only, have I sinned, and done this evil in Your sight—that You may be found just when You speak, and blameless when You judge.

Behold, I was brought forth in iniquity, and in sin my mother conceived me. Behold, You desire truth in the inward parts, and in the hidden part You will make me to know wisdom.

Purge me with hyssop, and I shall be clean; wash me, and I shall be whiter than snow. Make me hear joy and gladness, that the bones You have broken may rejoice. Hide Your face from my sins, and blot out all my iniquities.

Create in me a clean heart, O God, and renew a steadfast spirit within me (Ps. 51:1-10).

The greatest suffering any person could undergo is that which comes from rejecting the mercy and grace of a holy God. Confess your sins to God and turn from them. He will help you. And then make sure that you trust in Jesus Christ alone. Transfer your trust from yourself to the Savior, and be filled with the hope that only He can give.

JOB AND MORAL RELATIVISM

Job 11:1-6

After Job's many words, Job's friend Zophar spoke for the first time, and he didn't pull any punches. He virtually accused Job of lying:

> Should not the multitude of words be answered? and should a man full of talk be justified? Should thy lies make men hold their peace? and when thou mockest, shall no man make thee ashamed? For thou hast said, My doctrine is pure, and I am clean in thine eyes (Job 11:2-4, *KJV*).

Job was covered in excruciating boils to the point of being unrecognizable. His flesh was cracked open, he was covered in dust, he had lost his beloved children along with his riches and his dignity, his wife was telling him to curse God and die, and now, instead of comforting him, his friends were rubbing salt into his open and painful wounds. Zophar continued:

> But oh, that God would speak, and open His lips against you, that He would show you the secrets of wisdom! For they would double your prudence. Know therefore that God exacts from you less than your iniquity deserves (Job 11:5-6).

Zophar accused Job of being deceitful because Job maintained that he was unjustly suffering. Zophar then spoke on behalf of God, saying that if God treated Job according to his wickedness, things would be much worse than they already were. Keep in mind that God Himself had said of Job, "Have you considered My servant Job, that there is none like him on the earth, a blameless and upright man, one who fears God and shuns evil?" (Job 1:8).

EAR TICKLERS

The only time we should ever say "Thus says the Lord" is when we have His words written in Holy Scripture. If something isn't clearly laid out in Scripture, we dare not speak on behalf of God. As we will see in a future chapter of Job, Job's comforters didn't represent God correctly, and they came close to incurring God's wrath for their mistaken words.

There are many today who say that they represent God. Some have a platform; some don't. Like Job's friends, these people speak misleading words that often come wrapped in professed love and kindness. The problem is, their message is often clouded by the moral relativism that is so ingrained in our culture today. In other words, their perspective is based on external observations rather than on absolute truth as revealed in God's Word:

> I am a Christian, and I am in favor of gay marriage. The reason I am for gay marriage is because of my faith.
>
> What I see in the Bible's accounts of Jesus and his followers is an insistence that we don't have the moral authority to deny others the blessing of holy institutions like baptism, communion, and marriage. God, through the Holy Spirit, infuses those moments with life, and it is not ours to either give or deny to others. . . .
>
> My Take: the Bible doesn't condemn homosexuality. It is not our place, it seems, to sort out who should be denied a bond with God and the Holy Spirit of the kind that we find through baptism, communion, and marriage. The water will flow where it will.
>
> Intriguingly, this rule will apply whether we see homosexuality as a sin or not. The water is for all of us. We see

the same thing at the Last Supper, as Jesus gives the bread and wine to all who are there—even to Peter, who Jesus said would deny him, and to Judas, who would betray him.[1]

The citizens of this world latch particularly onto professing Christians who tickle their ears with what they want to hear, as this article about country music star Carrie Underwood shows us:

> The 29-year-old country superstar and former *American Idol*, who was raised Baptist, explained her position on the social debate in a recent interview with the *Independent*. "Above all, God wanted us to love others," she noted. "It's not up to me to judge anyone."
>
> Underwood, who is married to hockey star and fellow Christian Mike Fisher, says she and her husband attend a gay-friendly nondenominational church. "As a married person myself, I don't know what it's like to be told I can't marry somebody I love," she said. "I can't imagine how that must feel."
>
> "I definitely think we should all have the right to love, and love publicly, the people that we want to love."
>
> Underwood has been open about her faith throughout her career, and marked her first No. 1 hit with the religiously themed "Jesus Take the Wheel."[2]

It's obvious that both of these people are steering their own cars in the direction they want to take it and ignoring what God's Word says about homosexuality. This is moral relativism at its best. And it is a serious misrepresentation of the character of God.

Even though we are to proclaim the truth of God's Word, we must not vilify those who practice homosexuality as though they were sinning more badly than other people. The word "gospel" means "good news." The English language falls short of expressing the greatness of the news of the gospel. The gospel is phenomenally amazing news; it tells dying humanity that we can live forever! Look at who the good news is for:

Do you not know that the unrighteous will not inherit the kingdom of God? Do not be deceived. Neither fornicators, nor idolaters, nor adulterers, nor homosexuals, nor sodomites, nor thieves, nor covetous, nor drunkards, nor revilers, nor extortioners will inherit the kingdom of God (1 Cor. 6:9-10).

The gift of everlasting life is for fornicators, idolaters, adulterers (that includes those who lust—see Matt. 5:27-28), homosexuals, sodomites (male prostitutes), thieves, the covetous, drunkards, revilers (those who verbally attack others) and extortioners (those who extract money from people). Every one in any of those groups of people can be forgiven of their sins, escape the reality of Hell and find everlasting life! What sort of twisted and hate-filled person would I be if I purposely excluded homosexuals from the list?

I once had a couple of men come to my door and ask if I wanted to watch a video that showed that God was a mother. I told them that they could show me the video if they would let me film any conversation we had. One of them agreed, but he said that they could come back another day and film when they were "prepared." I said, "I think that you are already prepared. You wouldn't go knocking on the doors of strangers if you weren't prepared." Still, they didn't want to go on camera.

Then one of them began his prepared speech about God being a mother. He said that in Genesis 1 God said, "Let Us make man in Our image" (1:26). He said to notice that God is more than one, that He had made Adam in His image and then made Eve (a woman) in His image—therefore, God must be a woman as well as a man. I told my visitor that God is not a man and that any human characteristics given to Him in Scripture were examples of anthropomorphism.

When I asked the men how a person could be saved, they said that it was by keeping the commandments of God rather than by grace through faith (see Eph. 2:8-9). Their representation of God was not biblical. As they began to back away, I told them not to take their erroneous gospel to any of my neighbors, and I followed them down my driveway. I stood at the entrance with my arms folded, and as they walked down the road toward their car, one of them turned back and told me, "Don't worry; we're leaving." Some may think that my action was lacking in love. But look at Paul's words, spoken out of love, when it came to misrepresenting God:

> I marvel that you are turning away so soon from Him who called you in the grace of Christ, to a different gospel, which is not another; but there are some who trouble you and want to pervert the gospel of Christ. But even if we, or an angel from heaven, preach any other gospel to you than what we have preached to you, let him be accursed. As we have said before, so now I say again, if anyone preaches any other gospel to you than what you have received, let him be accursed (Gal. 1:6-9).

If you saw someone walking around your neighborhood offering people a sweet soda that you knew contained a deadly poison, would you feel that it was your moral duty to at least tell that person not to offer it to your neighbors? I hope so. Anything short of that would be unloving and unkind. Distorting the nature of God almost always manifests in the poison of "another gospel" that tells people that they don't need God's mercy.

The apostle John is called the apostle of love. He too used strong wording to warn people about false teaching: "If anyone comes to you and does not bring this doctrine, do not receive him into your house nor greet him; for he who greets him shares in his evil deeds" (2 John 1:10-11).

There are many, from the White House to the pulpit, who misrepresent God when it comes to the subjects of abortion and other significant moral issues. This is idolatry—making God in our own image. Others are so unthinking that they even deny God's existence so that they can enjoy sin with reckless abandon. But both atheism and idolatry have similar consequences: When people don't believe in God at all or they believe in a god who has no moral dictate, then for them anything goes; adultery isn't wrong, nor is lying, fornication, homosexuality, pedophilia, bestiality, stealing or legalized murder. Hitler legitimized slaughter in Germany, killing off six million Jews and others whom he considered to be "useless eaters," and he did it in the name of God. America has done a similar thing when it comes to abortion. We have legalized the killing of the unborn by dehumanizing them. And we reason that if unborn babies are not human, then it's okay to slaughter them.

This kind of reasoning has come about in our culture because of this thing that we call moral relativity. Instead of using the unchanging, objective standard of God's moral Law as our guide to what is right and wrong, we have embraced whatever *society* considers to be right and wrong. That's a slippery slope upon which to try to stand. With this mindset it will be only a matter of time until we fall.

One major reason we have this dilemma is that many pastors have failed to preach the character of God. They have neglected "the weightier matters of the law" (Matt. 23:23) and instead have tickled the ears of their hearers. Leonard Ravenhill rightly said that if Jesus had preached the same message that ministers preach today, He would never have been crucified. The Jews hated the Lord because of His uncompromising righteousness.

MAKING A 180

Sometimes what people need in order to turn from moral relativism to godly reasoning is an honest look at the truth. In 2011 I wrote a book called *Hitler, God and the Bible*, and I told the publishers that I would produce a video called *Hitler's Religion* to go with the book. As I worked on the project, I decided to forget the script and instead go out to the streets with a video camera to find out what people believed about Hitler. I could hardly believe what I found: 14 people—mainly university students—had no idea of the identity of Adolf Hitler. There were actually more than 14 who didn't know who Hitler was, but they were embarrassed to appear ignorant on camera. Then we were able to film some very colorful footage of myself being heckled in the open air, on two different occasions, by two very nasty neo-Nazis. We also obtained gripping footage of a Russian Jew who had lost loved ones to Nazis. We captured this while out on the street, with nothing prearranged. But the most amazing thing came from a mistake I made in one of my interviews.

Before I took to the streets to question people, I had wept my way through my research of the Holocaust for the book. One horrific incident I read about was of Nazis in Germany shooting hundreds of Jews and then burying them with a bulldozer. What broke my heart was that some of the Jews were still alive when they were buried. So I decided that the next time I interviewed a colorful university student, I would use this story to put him in a moral dilemma.

As I took to the streets with my camera, I found one such young person and began filming. I said to him, "It's 1943. A German officer has a gun pointed at you. He wants you to get into a bulldozer and drive it forward. In front of the bulldozer is a pit in which there are 300 Jews who have just been shot. Some of them are still alive. *The officer wants you to bury these people alive!* If you don't do what he says, he is going to kill you and then do the job himself. If you do what he says, he will let you live. *Would you drive the bulldozer forward?*"

This young man immediately said that he would never kill someone, because he was a compassionate person. It was then that I offhandedly and spontaneously said, "So how then do you feel about abortion?" The young man's demeanor changed, and he said he was for it. When I likened his attitude to the thinking of the Nazis, he became angry, and we crossed swords for about five minutes. He finally stormed off, and as I filmed him walking away, I looked down and saw that my camera was turned off.

I had been in direct sunlight, unable to see the screen, and had inadvertently switched the camera off at the beginning of the interview! It had been such a compelling exchange, and I was heartbroken that I hadn't captured it on film. So I determined to put more people into that scenario and see if the same thing happened. But the next time I did so, I went one step further and asked an extra question: "Isn't saying that abortion is a woman's right to choose the same as saying it was Hitler's right to choose to kill Jews?" To my amazement, that question caused a number of people to change their minds about abortion. These people went from being adamantly pro-abortion to pro-life in a matter of seconds.

I was so glad my camera had gotten switched off the first time I asked someone about abortion! We ended up with eight pro-abortion people becoming pro-life in seconds on camera simply because they were asked one question. We realized that we didn't have a *Hitler's Religion* video but rather a unique pro-life movie. So we changed the name of the movie to *180* and put it on a website called 180movie.com, and it went viral. What made *180* a unique movie was that it dealt with the error of moral relativity. A shifting moral compass sends the world in a wrong direction. It gives license for anyone to do what is right in his own eyes rather than what is right in God's eyes.

Here is one very strong response that we received from a viewer of *180*:

> You won't like me very much after reading this, but that's okay. You wanted my feedback, so here it is. I've had two abortions, and I am going for another one next week. If you really thought this would make me do a 180, you are sadly mistaken. Comparing what Hitler did to abortion is absurd. It's like trying to compare fire and water—you can't. This movie made me very angry. Wow, Ray, wow where did you get this idea? Pull it out of some hat with ideas people gave you? It's a horribly cruel trick to try and change people's minds. I am smarter than that. Using the god-factor means nothing. There is no god. There is no Heaven or Hell, and even if there was, I do not care. It's very judgmental to say there is never a reason to abort a pregnancy. This has got to be one of the worst films I have come across. Keep your god, and your religion. Quit trying to make people do a 180. It *is* a woman's choice.
> Linda

I responded to Linda's email and attached to my reply a picture of a member of our production crew holding a baby. The mother of that baby had watched *180* seven months earlier and had changed her mind about aborting her child. Here is what I wrote:

Linda. Thanks for writing and sharing your thoughts. I do appreciate that. Someone came to visit us yesterday who watched the movie last October (that's one of our production crew in the picture—holding the fruit of *180*). If you live in Southern California, please come and visit. We would take you to lunch, if you wish. Thanks again.

   Best wishes, Ray

A week later Linda responded:

Ray, I am not sure how much this will mean after the email I sent this past week, but I wanted to apologize for the insensitive and rude email directed towards you. Please forgive me. I get very angry easily. This movie made me extremely angry. I had no idea it was a Christian film.

   I am going to be completely honest here. I've been an atheist for most of my life, and as far as I'm concerned, I will die an atheist. I was not expecting an email back. I am 27 years old. Someone on the street was passing out the *180* movie last Monday. They asked me if I wanted one. I said, "What is it about?" They said, "About the Holocaust." I said, "Interesting" (I've always loved history).

   I brought it home and watched it on Wednesday. I was really liking the film until you started talking about abortion—like I said, I've had two previously. When you got to the part about God, I became even angrier. I hate anything that has to do with God, about God, by God . . . and this is another reason I was so hateful in my email.

   I did not tell you the truth in my last email. I was supposed to have the abortion this past Friday. Not this week. When I opened your email, with the attached picture of the beautiful baby . . . I could not get her out of my head. I tried pushing her out of my mind but couldn't. I said to myself, *Why do I feel so guilty?*

Friday I was driving with my boyfriend to the clinic, and the little smiling face of her was permanently cemented in my head. I said to my boyfriend, "I can't do this. I've got to go home." We turned around before we reached the clinic. I'm ashamed to admit it, but I started crying. My boyfriend thought I was nuts! I cried in bed the rest of that night. The memories of my past two abortions I had came flooding back. I would have two girls right now, who would be both 9 and 6. I knew they were going to be girls.

When you said, "It's okay to kill a baby in the womb when . . . ?" I couldn't answer it. Everything I emailed you was an attempt to make myself feel better. I really had no good reason for aborting the girls. I've put off the abortion for now, and I will tell you, I have never been confronted like that. I don't think that I can go through with a third abortion. I will admit this movie makes you think; in my case, it made me think too much . . . and I did not like it. I hated it. I hope you understand where I am coming from. I hope you'll excuse my hot-headed email.

I am sorry. Linda

The following email is another one of the many that we have received:

I completely did a 180! I've always thought abortion was okay in certain situations. I had an appointment at the abortion clinic today at 2:00 P.M. When my boyfriend found out I was pregnant, he had a fit and said, "Get rid of it." That made me cry. For months, he had pressured me, and many of my friends encouraged the abortion also. I gave in to the pressure, even though I didn't really want to have one! I thought it would make him love me again if I aborted the baby. I was selfish too, now that I look back.

Driving to the abortion clinic, I cried the whole way, not wanting to go through with it. I arrived at the abortion clinic, walked to its doors (oddly enough, I was about 20 minutes early), and I heard from behind me a woman yell out, "Ma'am, may I ask what you're going to do? Are you going in to have an abortion?"

I kind of stared at her, wondering why she was asking me that. I said, "Yes, I am, at 2:00 P.M."

She said, "Please don't do that. Would you come and talk with me first?" I hesitated, wondered where this was going. I walked over. She introduced herself. Her name was Anne. She had a laptop in her hands. She said, "I am so glad you came over to talk with me. I care about you and what you are about to do. Have you heard about the *180* movie?"

I said, "No."

She said, "Please, before you go into the clinic, will you watch this movie with me? It will explain some things that you might need to know."

I said, "Okay, I will watch it a little." She said great, and we sat down by her car. I watched the whole thing and missed my appointment. I had never heard anything like that! Wow! It broke me, and I realized how wrong I was.

I started crying again, and Anne put her hand on my shoulder. I thanked her that she was out there, because I didn't really want to go through with it in the first place. She told me, "I am a Christian, and God wants me to do this. This is my first day at this clinic. I wasn't going to go out today, but God prompted me to come here."

I said to Anne, "How many people have you talked to?"

She said, "No one else would stop and talk with me. You're the only one. God put me here for you."

I thought, *Wow! I didn't really want to go through with this, and look—someone was here who cared enough!* She showed love to someone who was going to abort her baby! It was her first day at this clinic! I have completely changed my mind about abortion!

Also, I have to tell you, at the end of the *180* movie, I had never heard about Jesus Christ in such a way. I asked Anne about Jesus and what Ray meant by what he said. She explained it to me again, took me through the Ten Commandments. After about an hour I repented of my sins (including the thought about murdering my baby and the sin of fornication) and trusted in Jesus to save me. All I can say is, "Amazing! Simply amazing! God put Anne there today!" What an amazing movie! This just makes me cry thinking about it all again!

Anne gave me her number and said, "Call to talk to me anytime you want." I can only imagine [what would have happened] if Anne wouldn't have been there and if this movie would have not been produced. I hope to send you a picture when my baby is born in October! You saved a life today, and I am grateful. Thank you, Jesus, Ray Comfort, Anne and all who worked on the *180* movie. It is a heart-changer! Amazing!

All the best, Kristi

Kristi wrote again after we contacted her. She said:

You have no idea how much this has impacted my life. Yesterday I would have committed the worst thing. I praise God for Anne. I will let her know what you said. I can only imagine what pain I would be going through now if I would have aborted my baby!

Could I ask you a favor? If you have not already done so, please consider sharing my email. People need to know how important it is that ladies go down to a local abortion clinic and show love to hurting women. It takes real courage to do what Anne did! It is all worth it! Anne was not holding a sign; she did not condemn me with her words. She just reached out in love—with the love of Jesus.

I literally had *no* hope, and she showed me the hope found in Jesus Christ! Having no one to support you is the hardest thing. Not having God in your life will make you do things you shouldn't do. You can't save everyone, but if you can change just one person's heart with the truth . . . then it is all worth it!!

All the work you put into this movie has been worth it! I had no idea this movie had over 3,000,000 views on YouTube! That is awesome! *Please* encourage people to go down to their local abortion clinic and do what Anne did— she did it in Jesus' name!! Don't give up! Keep sharing this awesome movie! God is great!

Blessings, my new friends, Kristi

MORAL RELATIVISM AND THE CONSCIENCE

One big problem with moral relativism is that eventually it dulls our sensibilities as to what is truly right or wrong. I was sitting in my office at our ministry when I heard what sounded like the painful groans of a poor woman experiencing the latter stages of childbirth—and who was also two weeks overdue with triplets and had been given no epidural. Whatever was happening was serious, because amidst the groans I could hear a distressed voice calling upon God for help. I dropped what I was doing and ran down the hall to the staff kitchen, not knowing what I was going to see. All I knew was that whatever it was, it had to be really bad.

When I looked into the kitchen, I saw Danny, a member of our staff, bent over the sink, frantically pouring water into his open mouth. He had a salt-shaker in his hand, a red flush on his face, sweat on his brow and tears in his pained eyes. Next to him stood our fix-it guy, Dave. But Dave didn't look as though he was in his normal confident fix-it mode. His eyes widened as he told me what had happened.

Danny had opened the refrigerator and accidentally touched a bottle of hot sauce. He saw some sauce on his finger and had intuitively licked it off. *Suddenly his mouth was on fire!* Unbeknownst to him the bottle was labeled "Dave's Gourmet Ghost Pepper Naga

Jolokia Hot Sauce." Pepper heat is measured by Scoville heat units, and the hottest chilies, such as habaneros and nagas, are rated over 200,000. This sauce was up there at about the heat level of the surface of the sun. *It was 650,000 Scoville heat units!*

I later checked out the website that sold the blistering substance, and one reviewer warned, "Yow, this stuff is hot . . . It will melt your face if you don't mix it." It looked as if Danny hadn't mixed it.

I knew that my friend Scotty used the sauce the way the average person uses ketchup on a hotdog, so I rushed downstairs and into the production studio where Scotty was setting up lights. I wildly said, "Danny accidentally got some hot sauce in his mouth, and he's going crazy with pain! What should he do?" Scotty smiled casually and said that all Danny could do was give it time. Scotty was a calm and cool veteran of the hottest of hot sauces, and many times I had watched in horror as he had bitten into incendiary peppers that I'm sure were created not to be eaten but to be used somehow in warfare. I surmised that Scotty had so scorched his unfortunate taste buds that they had left his mouth.

Such is the way of the hardened sinner and his conscience. A callous sinner thinks that he is getting away with sin, since guilt no longer registers in his senses. He doesn't feel the heat, because his conscience has been seared. But look at Scripture's warning about those who give themselves to sexual sin:

> Can a man take fire to his bosom, and his clothes not be burned? Can one walk on hot coals, and his feet not be seared? So is he who goes in to his neighbor's wife; whoever touches her shall not be innocent (Prov. 6:27-29).

It is not always easy to resist the persuasive arguments of others, particularly if they come from our friends, as they did in Job's case, and even more particularly if we are weakened by suffering or sorrow. But God's warning about sexual sin holds true for any kind of departure from the truth. God help us to stand firmly on His Word in our times of trial and testing.

JOB AND MESSIANIC PROPHECY

Job 16:1-14; 19:13; 30:9-10

Job and his friends continued to dialogue back and forth over the question of Job's guilt or innocence. Needless to say, Job's friends were not very encouraging to their friend who was suffering so terribly. Job's responses to them became more and more adamant and also more despondent. Job finally cried to his friends, "Miserable comforters are you all!" (Job 16:2).

But as Job spoke with frustration about his friends, he said something very interesting: "They gape at me with their mouth, they strike me reproachfully on the cheek, they gather together against me. God has delivered me to the ungodly, and turned me over to the hands of the wicked" (Job 16:10-11).

The Bible is full of statements like this one that actually say more than what is obvious in the immediate context. They are prophetic statements that apply not only to the situation in which they are spoken but also to an event that will take place in the future. These predictive verses prove the veracity of Scripture.

A cynical atheist once scornfully asked me what it would take for me to change my beliefs about the existence of God. It was a bright sunny day, so I said, "About as much as it would take for you to deny the existence of the sun." My analogy proved to be inadequate, because the cynic responded to me that he could think of a scenario in which he could believe that the sun was an illusion. I wasn't surprised.

I should have quoted something to him that I had written for atheists years ago. It more clearly gets the point across as to why I could never change my beliefs about God:

A Christian is someone who knows the Lord. Let me repeat that. Christians know the Lord. Actually know Him. Experientially. They know a Person, not a lifestyle. I'm talking about the God of the universe. They know Him. I will now personalize this, but I am speaking on behalf of everyone who knows the Lord. I don't *believe* that He exists. I *know* Him. Personally. I have a living relationship with the Creator. I talk to Him through prayer, and He guides me though His Word and by His Holy Spirit. I have known the Lord since April 24, 1972, at 1:30 in the morning.

Perhaps I'm not making myself clear, so I will try an analogy. It's like actually knowing someone. Personally. It's like having a friendship with Him—a 24-hour-a-day, 365-days-a-year, intimate relationship. . . . All the so-called "mistakes" in the Bible can't change that fact. All the hypocrisy committed by religious people in the past can't change it. All the atheists on God's earth saying that He doesn't exist doesn't change it in the slightest. Darwin's theory can't change it. The storms of this life can't change it. If I get cancer and die a horrible death, it doesn't change the fact that I know the Lord. I not only know Him, but I love Him. I love Him with all of my heart, soul, mind, and strength. He is my life. He's my joy, my Creator, my Savior, my Lord, and my God.[1]

The atheist was trying to show me that I was a closed-minded extremist—someone who was so blinded by "faith" that I wasn't open to reason, science, and plain common sense. However, I couldn't deny God's existence even if I wanted to. Creation cries out that there is a Creator. Conscience tells me that God created me with a sense of morality. The Ten Commandments show me that I'm a wicked sinner. And conversion brought me from an intellectual acknowledgment that God exists to a knowledge of Him personally.

The Bible has done nothing but make me grow in my convictions. It is sweet caloric icing on the cake of Christianity. And within that icing is an ingredient that stimulates the human brain: Bible prophecy.

It seems that all the suffering Job had undergone by this time had caused him to become a little paranoid. His three friends had left their own families and their everyday lives to sit with him in his pain. They had come to bring him comfort and to try to make sense of his terrible condition. Now they were wrong in their representation of the character of God and their assumptions as to why Job was suffering. But no one was gaping at him with their mouth or striking him on the cheek, as Job was complaining. And there was no evidence that God had turned Job over to the ungodly (see Job 16:10-11).

The phrase "They gape at me with their mouths" is an interesting one, because it is used word for word in Psalm 22:13, and that psalm is clearly messianic. Here it is in context:

> Many bulls have surrounded Me; strong bulls of Bashan have encircled Me. They gape at Me with their mouths, like a raging and roaring lion. I am poured out like water, and all My bones are out of joint; My heart is like wax; it has melted within Me (Ps. 22:12-14).

It is evident that with those words, Job was actually prophesying about the suffering that Jesus would one day undergo. Later Job would make further prophetic statements about the Messiah: "He has removed my brothers far from me, and my acquaintances are completely estranged from me" (Job 19:13), and "I am their taunting song; yes, I am their byword. They abhor me, they keep far from me; they do not hesitate to spit in my face" (Job 30:9-10). We see similar wording to this prophecy of Job in the book of Psalms:

They came round about me daily like water; they com-
passed me about together. Lover and friend hast thou put
far from me, and mine acquaintance into darkness (Ps.
88:17-18, *KJV*).

We see that Jesus Himself later predicted the same things when
He spoke to His disciples about His coming death and resurrection: "And they will mock Him, and scourge Him, and spit on Him,
and kill Him. And the third day He will rise again" (Mark 10:34).

After His resurrection Jesus appeared to two of His disciples.
The disciples didn't know that it was Jesus walking with them, and
so they talked to Him about the recent happenings in Jerusalem:
the fact that Jesus had been crucified and how some were saying
that He had risen from the dead:

> And when they found not his body, they came, saying, that
> they had also seen a vision of angels, which said that he
> was alive. And certain of them which were with us went to
> the sepulchre, and found it even so as the women had said:
> but him they saw not. Then he said unto them, O fools,
> and slow of heart to believe all that the prophets have spo-
> ken: Ought not Christ to have suffered these things, and
> to enter into his glory? And beginning at Moses and all
> the prophets, he expounded unto them in all the scrip-
> tures the things concerning himself (Luke 24:23-27, *KJV*).

The Scriptures prophesied of the coming Christ. They spoke
about Jesus. Way back in the writings of Moses and of all the
prophets were hidden what are often referred to as messianic
prophecies. We find them as gold nuggets, tucked into almost
every book in Holy Writ. There are so many, and they are so specific, that any Jew who believes the Old Testament will find himself at the feet of Jesus of Nazareth, acknowledging that Jesus is
indeed the promised Messiah. The problem is that many Jews ignore their Scriptures and instead embrace the more liberal writings of modern rabbis.

The Jewish Old Testament is unique among what are considered to be the world's sacred writings, because it predicted the future, and all of its predictions that have come true to date have proven to be 100 percent accurate. The 66 amazing books that make up the Old Testament (written between 1450 BC and 430 BC) contain hundreds of prophecies about an "anointed one" ("Messiah" in Hebrew). Following are those in the book of Genesis alone.[2]

Genesis	Prophecy	Fulfillment
The Messiah would be born of the "seed" of a woman.	Genesis 3:15	Luke 1:34-35
The Messiah would defeat Satan.	Genesis 3:15	1 John 3:8
The Messiah would suffer while reconciling men to God.	Genesis 3:15	1 Peter 3:18
The Messiah would be a descendant of Shem.	Genesis 9:26	Luke 3:36
The Messiah would be a descendant of Abraham.	Genesis 12:3	Matthew 1:1
The Messiah would be a descendant of Isaac.	Genesis 17:19	Luke 3:34
The Messiah would be a descendant of Abraham.	Genesis 18:17-18	Matthew 1:1
The Messiah would come for all nations.	Genesis 18:17-18	Acts 3:24-26
The Messiah would be a descendant of Isaac.	Genesis 21:12	Luke 3:34
The Messiah would be sacrificed on the same mountain on which God tested Abraham.	Genesis 22:14	Luke 23:33
The Messiah would be a descendant of Abraham.	Genesis 22:18	Galatians 3:16
The Messiah would come for all nations.	Genesis 22:18	Galatians 3:14
The Messiah would be a descendant of Isaac.	Genesis 26:4	Luke 3:34

Genesis	Prophecy	Fulfillment
The Messiah would be a descendant of Jacob.	Genesis 28:14	Luke 3:34
The Messiah would come for all people.	Genesis 28:14	Galatians 3:26-29
The Messiah would be a descendant of Judah.	Genesis 49:10	Luke 3:33
The Messiah would be a king.	Genesis 49:10	John 1:49

Like many other Old Testament biblical figures, Job was a "type" of the coming Christ. These types are seen in a number of people: Moses, the miracle-working deliverer who delivered his people from the bondage of Egypt, was like Jesus, the miracle-working deliverer who delivered His people from the bondage of sin and death (see Heb. 3:2). Joseph, who was betrayed by his own brethren and was unknown to them, was also like Jesus, who was betrayed by His own people and will remain unknown to Israel until His second coming (see John 1:10-11). Adam was a type of Christ (see Rom. 5:14), as were Jonah (see Matt. 12:38-41; Luke 11:29-32), Noah (see Gen. 5:29; Matt. 11:28) and David (see Ezek. 37:24; John 10:7-9).

The book of Job shows a man innocently suffering, forsaken by all, who was foreshadowing the innocent Lamb of God, who was forsaken by all and who suffered on our behalf so that we might be granted the gift of everlasting life. In speaking of Satan's attack on Job, Bible commentator Matthew Henry said:

> Permission is granted to Satan to make trial, but with a limit. If God did not chain up the roaring lion, how soon would he devour us! Job, thus slandered by Satan, was a type of Christ, the first prophecy of whom was, that Satan should bruise his heel, and be foiled.[3]

These prophecies from the book of Job and from other places in the Old Testament were fulfilled nearly 2,000 years ago. In chapter 21 of this book, we will look at books in the Bible that contain predictions of the future that are being fulfilled at this very moment.

JOB AND LADY GAGA

Job 21:1–22:30

Have you ever wondered why it is that Christians often get sick and die but that God allows the wicked to live long and happy lives? Those who reject God are in many cases prosperous, healthy, blasphemous, filthy-mouthed and famous. On top of their success, they have the adulation of this sinful world. When they want to say something, they have a platform, and the world listens to them; thus their godless and sin-filled agenda is furthered.

As Job sat in his misery, he wondered the same thing:

Why do the wicked live and become old, yes, become mighty in power? Their descendants are established with them in their sight, and their offspring before their eyes. Their houses are safe from fear, neither is the rod of God upon them. Their bull breeds without failure; their cow calves without miscarriage. They send forth their little ones like a flock, and their children dance. They sing to the tambourine and harp, and rejoice to the sound of the flute (Job 21:7-12).

Job asked why the "rod of God" wasn't upon the wicked. He now believed that he was under the chastening rod. It had swiftly come down upon his head and taken all that he had. The wicked, Job felt, were powerful, happy and healthy. But Job went a step further in his thinking, meditating on the attitude of the wicked and on their eventual fate:

> They spend their days in wealth, and in a moment go down to the grave. Yet they say to God, "Depart from us, for we do not desire the knowledge of Your ways. Who is the Almighty, that we should serve Him? And what profit do we have if we pray to Him?" (Job 21:13-16).

The wicked may enjoy wealth and safety in this life, but they know that one day they are going to die, and yet they still don't seek God. They don't want Him. Actually, none of us does. Despite the fact that many people testify that they have always loved the Lord, the Scripture tells us, "There is none who understands; there is none who seeks after God" (Rom. 3:11). A friend of mine who had been brought up in a Christian home but had rebelled in his late teens epitomized this to me. In his book *SEAL of God*, Chad Williams tells the story of how he became a Navy SEAL.

As a young adult, Chad was living with his Christian parents but partying heavily. Early one morning he returned home drunk and covered with someone else's blood. His parents had had enough, and they told Chad that he had to leave home. Chad put it this way: "I was no longer welcome in their home if I intended to continue on in the drinking, fighting and exploiting their hospitality as I simply used their household as a place to sleep off the night's intoxication."

However, he didn't have anywhere to store a large keg of beer he had hidden in their garage, so he devised a plan to sneak the beer keg out his parents' home. He asked his mom and dad if he could attend a Christian meeting with them that night. He took his girlfriend and briefed her as to what would happen: the preacher would preach, then he would ask for a show of hands, and people would go to the front of the church. Chad told his girlfriend, "Whatever you do, don't raise your hand!" That would mean that she would have to go down to the front and get prayer, and it would keep them longer at the meeting. He wanted to get home to get that keg of beer before his parents left the church. But much to his girlfriend's surprise, *Chad* raised his sinful hand when challenged by the preacher, and he went to the front and was soundly saved.

This epitomizes true conversion. Jesus said that no one comes to the Son unless the Father draws him. We human beings are so sinful that it takes the grace of God to bring us to Himself. We all have some hidden keg of beer. Just as Job mused, in our hearts we blindly say to God, "Depart from us. We don't desire knowledge of Your ways." Even though God has given us eyes, ears, food, family and life itself, we say, "Who is God that I should serve Him, and what would I get out of it if I did?"

GOOD NEWS FROM DOWN UNDER

God does sometimes, however, allow His rod to fall on the ungodly. When wicked people have spent their lives hardening their hearts, God lets death seize on them. Despite what he had already said, Job went on to warn, "For the wicked are reserved for the day of doom; they shall be brought out on the day of wrath" (Job 21:30).

I do not hear too much good news from my home country of New Zealand—what with the declining international economy and the killer earthquake in the city of Christchurch back in 2011 with its ensuing misery. But some really good news did come along in June 2012. I heard that as the popular singer Lady Gaga was in the city of Auckland singing her anti-Christian song "Judas," a backup singer accidentally smacked her in the head with a large pole.

Well, actually, the good news is that she only suffered a concussion. But I remember hoping that the incident would knock some sense into her—that maybe she would think twice about singing her love song to Judas, in which she croons, "I'll bring him down, bring him down, down, a king with no crown, king with no crown," obviously referring to Jesus. She also sings, "In the most biblical sense, I am beyond repentance. . . . Jesus is my virtue, and Judas is the demon I cling to."

There is more good news—for Lady Gaga. She need not cling to demons, and she's not beyond repentance. The Bible says, "Whoever calls on the name of the LORD shall be saved" (Rom. 10:13). No one is beyond repentance while he is still breathing. God is *very* patient with even the worst of us.

Remember that Job warned, "For the wicked are reserved for the day of doom; they shall be brought out on the day of wrath" (Job 21:30). That's the message we should be preaching—that all human beings are wicked in God's eyes and are under His wrath (see John 3:36) but that God is rich in mercy and has provided us a Savior. Health-and-wealth prosperity preachers have another message, and they may have gotten their cue from perhaps the first health-and-wealth preacher—one of Job's comforters, Eliphaz the Temanite:

> Is not your wickedness great, and your iniquity without end? For you have taken pledges from your brother for no reason, and stripped the naked of their clothing. You have not given the weary water to drink, and you have withheld bread from the hungry. But the mighty man possessed the land, and the honorable man dwelt in it. You have sent widows away empty, and the strength of the fatherless was crushed. Therefore snares are all around you, and sudden fear troubles you, or darkness so that you cannot see; and an abundance of water covers you (Job 22:5-11).

What he was saying makes sense. Job had been healthy, wealthy and happy. But now he was poor, sick and miserable. To Eliphaz, Job's riches and wealth had been signs of God's blessing. Obviously, he thought, Job had lost the blessing of God because he had somehow angered Him. So Eliphaz took a calculated stab at the things he thought Job secretly may have done to anger God. Job had:

1. Taken unwarranted pledges from brethren to make money
2. Allowed the weary to go thirsty
3. Allow people to go hungry
4. Denied widows and orphans the necessities of life

Eliphaz believed that these omissions were the secret sins of Job. He thought that Job's wickedness was great and his iniquity without end. What had happened to Job wouldn't have happened to a man who had God's blessing on his life. Eliphaz went on:

> Now acquaint yourself with Him, and be at peace; thereby good will come to you. Receive, please, instruction from His mouth, and lay up His words in your heart. If you return to the Almighty, you will be built up; you will remove iniquity far from your tents. Then you will lay your gold in the dust, and the gold of Ophir among the stones of the brooks. Yes, the Almighty will be your gold and your precious silver; for then you will have your delight in the Almighty, and lift up your face to God. You will make your prayer to Him, He will hear you, and you will pay your vows. You will also declare a thing, and it will be established for you; so light will shine on your ways. When they cast you down, and you say, "Exaltation will come!" then He will save the humble person. He will even deliver one who is not innocent; yes, he will be delivered by the purity of your hands (Job 22:21-30).

In other words, he who has God's smile will be healthy, wealthy and happy. But Eliphaz was wrong.

God forbid that any of us should fall into the easy error of thinking that this life's blessings are signs of God's approval. If they are, then the Mafia and many other villains who are rich and happy have God's approval. So do the many millionaires and billionaires throughout the world who live godless lives. Job's friends were in error—but so was Job. We are about to see that he had one big sin of which he was not at all aware.

JOB AND IDOLATRY

Job 23:1-17

Have you ever studied Hinduism's gods? Some of them have multiple arms; another may have an elephant trunk for a nose. These figures of the gods represent some beneficial trait of the gods' character. If we were to create a physical idol to represent America's image of God, the likeness would probably have large hands made of gold to represent the prosperity that we think God wants to give everyone and a smiling face to signify that He will make our lives problem-free and happy. All we have to do is burn some sacrificial incense—by giving an offering to the TV preacher who owns the idol—to put our idol to work.

There is another characteristic that could be added. We could add a tear to the image's eyes to show that God is crying because sinners ignore Him. Christians who are sincere but who lack any depth of biblical theology often give this sad image to the world. It is a wrong image of God.

Perhaps believers get this thought from remembering that Jesus wept over Jerusalem. But when God became a human being in Christ, He subjected Himself to human emotions and weaknesses. When Jesus was incarnated, He became tired, fearful, hungry and thirsty, and He experienced pain. However, nothing in Scripture tells us that God gets tired, thirsty, hungry or fearful or that He suffers physical pain as do human beings.

Or perhaps people get the thought that God cries over sinners from Jeremiah 14:17-18, where God says to the prophet:

Therefore you shall say this word to them: "Let my eyes flow with tears night and day, and let them not cease; for the virgin daughter of my people has been broken with a mighty stroke, with a very severe blow. If I go out to the field, then behold, those slain with the sword! And if I enter the city, then behold, those sick from famine! Yes, both prophet and priest go about in a land they do not know."

Modern Christianity often makes God out to be a helpless and powerless entity who has lost sovereign reign over the universe, is subject to the whimsical dictates of this fallen creation, and is just one big emotional basket case because sinners ignore Him. The Scriptures tell us that our Creator has a deep sadness at the death of the wicked and that He prefers mercy to justice. He is empathetic, compassionate, loving, good and kind beyond our deepest understanding, and while we *can* grieve the Lord with our sins, there is no biblical justification for us to believe that God is sitting in Heaven physically crying because He is dejected over humanity.

While the sensitive Christian may see such an image of God as one of love and compassion, in the eyes of the ungodly, the image is insipid and even ugly. Hurricanes and tornadoes tear lives apart. Disease kills millions. Earthquakes crush families. And God does not prevent any of these things or help the victims of these catastrophes—He just cries about them.

SERIOUS SINS

If we want the sinner to see what God is like, we must represent the Lord by being uncompromisingly faithful to Holy Scripture. Job's comforters misrepresented the character of God, but they had an excuse for their ignorance: they didn't have the light of God's Word to reveal their Creator. Their idol had been created by their moral intuition and in their imaginations. They instinctively knew that God was righteous, that He required moral accountability; and they therefore wrongly imagined that Job had angered God through serious secret sins.

Scripture, however, gives us light, and it is that light that we are to shine into a dark and spiritually ignorant world. God is angry with the wicked every day. His wrath abides on them. Every time they sin, they store up His wrath (see Rom. 2:5). God is to be feared, because He has the power to cast body and soul into Hell. Such biblical preaching is alarming in the truest sense of the word, and it can awaken sinners to flee from the wrath to come. This is because it is the fear of the Lord that causes men to depart from sin. But talk of a god whose supreme object is to make sinners rich and happy or one who is quietly crying on his heavenly throne does nothing but comfort sinners in their aberrant state.

None of us this side of Heaven has any real concept of God's holiness. The Scriptures say that no man has ever seen God nor can see Him. If we stood in God's presence, His holiness would instantly kill us. When Moses asked to see God's glory, the Lord told him that he couldn't see Him and live. So God hid Moses in the cleft of a rock and let His "goodness" pass by. Moses was then allowed to look at the place where God had been. The Bible says that when Moses came down from the holy mountain, Israel could not even look at his face, because he had looked at God's back (see Exod. 33:18-23). The reason God's goodness would kill us if we saw it is because we cannot separate His goodness from His justice, and His justice demands retribution for evil.

For about three years a man named Willie always heckled me when I preached the gospel outdoors. He would angrily yell, "When I stand before God I'm going to say, 'What about this Ray Comfort?' Then I will spit in the face of God!" Willie dropped dead of a heart attack at age 38. While we have no idea if God lost patience with Willie, we do have precedent in Scripture for God losing His forbearance with certain people:

> Then He spoke a parable to them, saying: "The ground of a certain rich man yielded plentifully. And he thought within himself, saying, 'What shall I do, since I have no room to store my crops?' So he said, 'I will do this: I will pull down my barns and build greater, and there I will

store all my crops and my goods. And I will say to my soul, "Soul, you have many goods laid up for many years; take your ease; eat, drink, and be merry." ' But God said to him, 'Fool! This night your soul will be required of you; then whose will those things be which you have provided?'

"So is he who lays up treasure for himself, and is not rich toward God" (Luke 12:16-21).

Like Willie, Job wanted to speak with God. He had a few questions for the Almighty. His questions weren't blasphemous as Willie's were, but they came from a lack of understanding on Job's part, as we will see later. Job's words reveal that he had an incorrect image of God. He bewailed:

Oh, that I knew where I might find Him, that I might come to His seat! I would present my case before Him, and fill my mouth with arguments. I would know the words which He would answer me, and understand what He would say to me. Would He contend with me in His great power? No! But He would take note of me. There the upright could reason with Him, and I would be delivered forever from my Judge (Job 23:3-7).

Job's lack of understanding is reasonable. He didn't have verses of Scripture to tell him that the eye of the Lord is in every place, beholding the evil and the good (see Prov. 15:3).

God sees everything all at once. He sees the inner core of the sun. If that seems beyond impossible, ask yourself who it was who made the sun, and if it was God who made it, then surely He can see what He made. God sees the innermost atom of the largest planet that is spinning through space, a trillion light years from the earth. The Lord has followed the flight of every sparrow and listened to every song that flowed from their chirping beaks. This is because He gave the bird the ability to sing each morning. God also saw the thought life of Moses, of Napoleon, of William Shakespeare and of Shakespeare's grandmother's cat's fleas. He has seen the thought life of every one of the billions of human beings He has created down through the ages. The Lord has witnessed every single crime against His Law, and He has stored up His just wrath against every single perpetrator.

In Psalm 139 King David was blown away by the incomprehensible thoughts of God:

> You have searched me and known me. You know my sitting down and my rising up; You understand my thought afar off. You comprehend my path and my lying down, and are acquainted with all my ways. For there is not a word on my tongue, but behold, O LORD, You know it altogether. You have hedged me behind and before, and laid Your hand upon me. Such knowledge is too wonderful for me; it is high, I cannot attain it (Ps. 139:1-6).

Every one of us (in our unregenerate state) is an idolater. Our perception of God is inaccurate. Ask the average unconverted person what he or she thinks God is like, and you will get a variety of unbiblical images—from an old man in the sky, to a heavenly butler whose chief end is to cater to the wants of humanity, to someone who sits blindly in Heaven, totally oblivious to what's happening here on earth.

THE GOLD

Yet Job, despite his wrong image of the Lord, was strides ahead of the best of us. He knew that God was holy, and he trusted God even in the face of death. Job also saw an end to the misery in which he sat. He said, "When He has tested me, I shall come forth as gold" (Job 23:10). That's commendable, because even with the knowledge that we have as Christians, it's hard for us to see what good could possibly come through any Job-like experience we might face. When we are in the lion's den, it is natural for us to think about the teeth of the lions and the way to get away from them.

Many years ago I went through an experience that left me dev-
astated for five years. For an entire year of that time I couldn't even
have a meal with my family. I had agoraphobia (commonly called
"panic attacks"). As difficult as it was, that horrific experience has
given me empathy for those who are suffering, and that's a precious virtue for any Christian to possess.

A man who was a CPA read a book that I wrote on how to overcome panic attacks, and he contacted me because he was experiencing attacks and worse. This man was suffering from serious
insomnia. This was because his first attack had come "out of the
black"—when he had been deeply asleep. The man suddenly awoke
in the early hours of the morning, filled with terror, something he
had never experienced before. That affected him psychologically so
that he was fearful of sleep, and so he went for months addicted to
sleeping pills, which then produced side effects in him. In time, however, this man stopped taking the pills and gained victory over both
the insomnia and the panic attacks. When I said, "It sure does give
you empathy for other's sufferings," he responded with a sober and
sincere voice. "Oh, Ray," he said, "it really does." He then said that
his experience had made him think differently and that he had begun to treat people with a very gentle understanding and comfort.
If you are in the lion's den (see Dan. 6), trust God, and look past the
teeth of the lions to the precious gold that God sees in your life.

Job's trust, even in the midst of his questions and his suffering,
was rooted in his healthy fear of God:

> Therefore I am terrified at His presence; when I consider
> this, I am afraid of Him. For God made my heart weak,
> and the Almighty terrifies me (Job 23:15-16).

He was where we should be. We should fear God and therefore
trust Him. If we do neither, we are in violation of the command
of Jesus:

> And I say to you, My friends, do not be afraid of those who
> kill the body, and after that have no more that they can

do. But I will show you whom you should fear: Fear Him who, after He has killed, has power to cast into hell; yes, I say to you, fear Him! (Luke 12:4-5).

THE FEAR OF GOD AND OBEDIENCE

The fear of the Lord, as we have just seen, produces the obedience of trust. And it is trust in God that helps us deal with our wrong fears. This is important, because God commands us to reach out to the lost—and an unhealthy fear of man rather than a holy fear of God often keeps us from doing that. The apostle Paul said, "Knowing, therefore, the terror of the Lord, we persuade men" (2 Cor. 5:11). If we do not know the terror of the Lord, we will sit on a pew and sing praises to the God we refuse to obey. But if we have a right concept of His nature—if we have a correct image of God—it will produce more than awe that results in worship. It will motivate us to stand up and witness and preach the gospel to this dying world.

What motivates us more: the fear of man or the fear of God? If we fear man more than we fear God, then we don't see God in truth. We see the Lord as less than a man—and this is proven by whose will we obey. A. W. Tozer said, "An idol of the mind is as offensive to God as an idol of the hand."[1]

Some of us are like Job's comforters. We see people in terrible need, and we don't say anything to them. All around us people are dying—we have found everlasting life, so how dare we remain silent? Maybe it's not convenient to actually share the gospel, but we can always carry gospel tracts that show the way of salvation.

I was in a large store once when I saw an elderly man struggling to get into a motorized shopping cart. I walked up to him and asked, "May I help you, sir?" This man was probably in his early nineties, well dressed and very clean looking. He gently nodded, and so I grabbed his arm and helped him. As he sat down, he earnestly said, "It's horrible, getting old . . ."

I asked, "Sir, are you a Christian?"

"I hope so," he replied.

I took one of our trillion-dollar-bill tracts from my pocket, turned it over and said, "Make sure you read the back of this. It tells you how to get everlasting life. I hope the print isn't too small."[2] He took it, gestured to his top pocket and said, "I have a magnifying glass in my pocket." I also gave him a "Thank You for Listening to Me" tract. This one expounds principles of Christian growth. The whole encounter lasted a mere 30 seconds between two people who were headed in different directions. It may have been a divine encounter and will hopefully result in someone finding everlasting life.

Catherine Booth said this regarding the many believers who are weak and unstable:

> Here is the reason why we have such a host of stillborn, sinewless, ricketty, powerless spiritual children. They are *born of half-dead* parents, a sort of sentimental religion which does not take hold of the soul, which has no depth of earth, no grasp, no power in it, and the result is a sickly crop of sentimental converts. Oh! the Lord give us a real, robust, living, hardy, Christianity, full of zeal and faith, which shall bring into the kingdom of God lively, well-developed children, full of life and energy, instead of these poor sentimental ghosts that are hopping around us.[3]

The co-founder of the Salvation Army was contrasting those who fear God with those who don't. Charles Spurgeon said:

> Now idolatry is a sin of the most heinous character; it is not an offense against men it is true, but it is an intolerable offense against the majesty of God. . . . I confess I would almost rather be charged with a religion that extenuated murder, than with one that justified idolatry. Murder, great as the offense is, is but the slaying of man; but idolatry is in its essence the killing of God; it is the attempt to thrust the Eternal Jehovah out of his seat, and

to foist into His place the work of his own hand, or the creature of my own conceit.[4]

A lack of obedience is the fruit of a false conversion, and a false conversion always traces itself back to the sin of idolatry.

I 3

JOB AND TRUST

Job 13:15; 19:25-27

What is the purpose of human existence? This is one of the hardest questions for the ungodly to answer. As far as those who do not know Christ understand, they are born for no reason, they live with no purpose, and they die with no hope.

Ask the average university student about human origin, and all he will say is that we are the product of a random bang, that we are primates with no purpose, and that death is probably the end of life. There may be a Heaven; there may be a Hell. But the unsaved don't know, and many of them are so busy with the pleasures of this life that they don't think about God or the next life:

> For the wicked boasts of his heart's desire; he blesses the greedy and renounces the LORD. The wicked in his proud countenance does not seek God; God is in none of his thoughts (Ps. 10:3-4).

Of all the issues that we should consider in life, the most important should be our own individual survival. We should be like Christian in *Pilgrim's Progress* who ran out of his house, crying, "Life, life, eternal life!" and seeking desperately to find salvation. Even for those who are atheists and those who embrace evolution, self-preservation should be humanity's most basic primal instinct. When Evangelist asked the pilgrim in Bunyan's famous book why he was so distressed, Christian answered:

"Sir, I perceive, by the book in my hand, that I am condemned to die, and after that to come to judgment; and I find that I am not willing to do the first, nor able to do the second."

Then said Evangelist, "Why not willing to die, since this life is attended with so many evils?"

The man answered, "Because, I fear that this burden that is upon my back will sink me lower than the grave, and I shall fall into Tophet. And Sir, if I be not fit to go to prison, I am not fit to go to judgment, and from thence to execution; and the thoughts of these things make me cry."

Then said Evangelist, "If this be thy condition, why standest thou still?"

He answered, "Because I know not whither to go."

Then he gave him a parchment roll, and there was written within, "Fly from the wrath to come."

The man therefore read it, and looking upon Evangelist very carefully, said, "Whither must I fly?"

Then said Evangelist, (pointing with his finger over a very wide field) "Do you see yonder wicket-gate?"

The man said, "No."

Then said the other, "Do you see yonder shining light?"

He said, "I think I do."

Then said Evangelist, "Keep that light in your eye, and go up directly thereto, so shalt thou see the gate; at which, when thou knockest, it shall be told thee what thou shalt do."

So I saw in my dream that the man began to run. Now he had not run far from his own door when his wife and children, perceiving it, began to cry after him to return; but the man put his fingers in his ears, and ran on crying, Life! life! eternal life! So he looked not behind him, but fled towards the middle of the plain.[1]

The pilgrim's reason for seeking God was the knowledge of his sin. He cried, "This burden that is upon my back will sink me lower than the grave." Nothing makes a sinner cry "Life! Life! Eternal life!" as does the knowledge that he has sinned against a holy God and will have to face the Lord on Judgment Day. So our task is (with the help of God) to bring the issue of eternity to the thoughts of the ungodly.

After more than 40 years of sharing my faith, I have found that asking what happens to people after they die to be a wonderful key in unlocking these thoughts. Very few people are offended by it, because it doesn't mention sin, God, Jesus, the Bible, Heaven or Hell. It's a gentle feeler to see if they are open to thoughts about God. Most answer that they have the hope of seeing Heaven, and that response dissipates the fear of rejection and opens the door to further conversation.

TRUST AND BANKS

Perhaps you are in the middle of a Job experience. You picked up this book because you are in despair. You are hearing whispers of "Curse God and die." Perhaps suicide has crept into your mind. Don't listen to the enemy. The devil came to kill, steal and destroy (see John 10:10). All he offers is death. Instead, if you want to live, listen to the life-giving words of the Word of God.

One of those words came from the mouth of Job as he experienced his own horrible temptation to despair. But even though he was wracked with pain, discouraged by his wife and accused by his friends, Job showed his faith in God by stating these words that are almost certainly the most central to the story of Job: "Though He slay me, yet will I trust Him" (Job 13:15).

This verse shows us the first of two things we must do to survive the lion's den in which we sometimes find ourselves. The first thing we must do, as we have already talked about many times in this book, is to put our faith in God, to trust the Lord with all our heart. This isn't hard to do. If anyone thinks that it is, he is mistaken. Faith in God has nothing to do with believing that He exists. We *know* that He exists because of creation. It didn't make itself; all around us we see the genius of His handiwork. No, faith in God goes beyond believing in His existence—it extends to believing in His promises and then acting on them.

Let me give you an example of trust. Money is something we learn about as children. As we grow, it slowly dawns on us that money makes the world go around. When we give money to people, they give us things. Without money, we cannot get the items we want. If we want a new toy, we need money. If we want food at the supermarket, we need money. As we grow older, the time comes when we earn our own cash by doing odd jobs around the home. As time further passes, we work, save and buy a car using money that we put into a bank account.

There was a time when money was a piece paper that represented a government promise. Now we buy things using numbers—account numbers, debit and credit card numbers, bank balances. These numbers allow us access to the money that we have in the bank. We trust that the bank keeps an accurate account of our numbers. We trust that we can bank on the bank. It is that easy. If we didn't trust the bank, we would remove our wealth-representing numbers and put them somewhere else—with a bank that we could trust. The entire process of banking is built on trust.

Our relationship with God is built on this same kind of trust. It is trust in God that provides the means of exchange between Him and humanity.

NOT FOR A SECOND

I have trusted God since April 24, 1972. I have never doubted Him once in more than 40 years, not for a second. That may sound like an arrogant and boastful statement, but it's not. Let me explain.

In more than 40 years of marriage, I have never doubted my wife, *not for a second*. I trust her implicitly. I never worry about her being unfaithful or lying to me or stealing from me. Such thoughts are ridiculous. I am not concerned about such things because I know my wife and love her. If I didn't trust her, it would be an insult to her integrity. Now talking about my trust in Sue isn't arrogance at all. It may be a boast, but it's a wonderful boast, because it gives honor to my wife—and the same applies to trust in God. If you don't trust God, then it means that you think He's not trustworthy. If you do trust Him, you give Him instant praise.

If God's Word says that *all* things are working together for my good, I believe it. Through faith, I can rest in that promise. It was because He trusted in God that Jesus was able to sleep in a violent storm. The unbelieving disciples were terrified, but Jesus so trusted the Father that He snoozed on a pillow. If we lack peace in the storms of life, it's because we don't trust God, even though He is perfect in character and has impeccable integrity.

It's easy for us to look at the amazing faith of Job and to admire him. How many people do we know who would truly say, "Though He slay me, yet will I trust Him"? Yet even though it is measurably admirable for a person to trust God while in terrible pain, for us to focus on Job's trust in God is to miss the main point. If we came across a person who had the sort of faith in any man or woman that Job had in God, it makes far more sense for us to enquire about the person who is *being* so trusted—"Who is this incredible person for someone to have such faith in them?" When I speak of trusting my wife, your thoughts of admiration should go to her rather than to me. Sinful Job had caught merely a glimpse of the faithfulness of his Creator, even in the darkness of death itself, and he knew that God could be trusted. Those who understand this amazing truth will switch on a bright light in their own personal blackness. Jesus said, "I am the Light of the world. He who follows Me [in this life and in the next] will not be walking in the dark, but will have the Light which is Life" (John 8:12, *AMP*).

When I think of examples of those who have shown strong faith, I often think of Gwen Wilkerson, wife of the famous preacher David Wilkerson. When she was a 32-year-old mother, Gwen was diagnosed with cancer. Later her two precious daughters also faced cancer while they were still relatively young. Behind the scenes of her husband's prominent and successful ministry, Gwen and her daughters endured 16 surgeries and 9 cancers, much to the anguish of David Wilkerson.

In 2011 Gwen was seriously injured and her beloved husband tragically killed in a terrible car accident. In a moment of time, she lost the love of her life as well as her health, and she found herself in a broken body, wracked with unspeakable pain. So where was God in this? Where was His protecting hand? Didn't He love the Wilkersons? Had they done something to lose God's favor? Those who don't understand the book of Job will ask questions like these and will come to their own conclusions. But those who fear God and who understand sound doctrine will say that God in His infinite wisdom allowed this horror—but that He is still good and has our best interests in mind. We may not know why God allows such suffering, but He does, and we can conquer our endless questions through trust in Him.

You may not have the ability to sing or play a musical instrument. You may have been left in the dust when it comes to playing sports or to the ability to make money. Some people have these kinds of abilities, and some don't. However, there is one aspect of life that is a level playing field for all humanity. *Any* of us can exercise faith in God, *because trust is not dependent on our ability but upon God's faithfulness.*

So the first thing we should do when we are in the middle of a dark experience is to affirm our faith in God. We do that by first confessing our sins, and then we confess our trust in the Savior. We can say to the Lord with Job, "Though You slay me, yet will I trust You." And we need to keep saying it until we mean it. There is good reason for this, because the day will come when we will pass through the door of death, and we will need to have this truth fully established in our hearts. Repetition of it isn't just a mental exercise. If we can get to a point of having the faith of Job, we will be doing ourselves a great favor.

Following is a faith-filled affirmation of trust in God. Read it, memorize it and speak it out loud again and again until it becomes your heartfelt conviction:

Father, I know that You created me (see Gen. 1:27) and that You know my sitting down and my rising up (see Ps. 139:2).

You are acquainted with all my ways (see Ps. 139:3), and You proved Your great love for me on the cross of Calvary (see Rom. 5:8). I also know that anything that comes my way comes only by Your loving permission (see Job 2:3-6).

Your Word promises that all things work together for my good, because I love You and I'm called according to Your purposes (see Rom. 8:28). I trust You with all my heart and will not lean on my own understanding (see Prov. 3:5). I will not fear the future (see Ps. 56:4). I will not fear suffering or even death (see Rom. 8:35-37).

From my heart I say with Job, "Though He slay me, yet will I trust Him" (Job 13:15). This is because nothing—not even death itself—can separate me from You or from Your everlasting love (see Rom. 8:38-39). I therefore thank You in and for all things (see Eph. 5:20), I praise Your holy name, and I rejoice in You (see Hab. 3:17-18) because You are my very life (see Col. 3:4). You, not the enemy, hold my breath in Your mighty hands (see Ps. 104:29). In Jesus' name I pray and affirm these things (see Col. 3:17). Amen.

WHAT IS YOUR PROBLEM?

All around us people are going through painful Job experiences—and some of these people are Christians. Many of these believers, although tasting the bitter cup of suffering, overcome their condition through faith—and through putting their faith into action. They have learned that in addition to trusting God, another thing they can do in the midst of a fiery trial is to get their eyes off themselves. Think of Aimee Copeland, the 24-year-old woman who in 2012 was stricken by a terrifying flesh-eating disease. She lost a leg and both of her hands. When asked to give a statement, she said, "I feel blessed . . . I feel unique . . . I have a unique opportunity that God has basically given me a challenge."[2]

Getting our eyes off ourselves is not easy for us to do, but the reality is that all around us are unsaved people who could be snatched into a very real Hell in the span of a heartbeat. This brings any trial we are going through into perspective. Nothing could be more horrific than waking up in Hell. We may feel the bitter cold while we are in the lifeboat, but we know that we are saved. All around us, however, are people in the ice-cold water, about to be pulled under the surface and to sink to their deaths. I find that nothing warms my soul like reaching out to the lost and seeing them pulled to the safety of the Savior. So there is another reason for us to apply ourselves to the irksome task of evangelism.

Back in 1982, when I was going through some of my darkest experiences due to my panic attacks, I decided that I was not going to let the enemy paralyze me.[3] I was going to continue to reach out to the lost, because their problem was much bigger than mine. I was having a tiny taste of Hell on earth, but I had the hope that there was a light at the end of my tunnel. I clung to hope. But those who die in their sins will not have a hope in Hell. There will be no end to their terror.

I received this moving email from a dear brother in Christ whose desire to share Christ with others in spite of his limitations and anxieties inspired me:

> I'm 18 years old, and I have cerebral palsy. I'm in a wheelchair, and I use a special computer I access using my eyes. Despite my difficulties ... I'm convinced that it's my destiny to preach the gospel. I know people will listen to me, because they are interested in my disability, so I figure the most important thing I can tell them is the gospel. . . . I also have trouble with fear. I can stand a little bit with assistance, but I have a very weak left leg. When I'm standing, I'm afraid I'll fall. I also get really anxious sometimes for no reason. I want to preach the gospel and serve Christ, but I'm afraid these issues will slow me down. Do you have any suggestions for me? —JG

I wrote back the following thoughts:

JG, I have often thought what I would do if I ended up in a wheelchair: I would have someone help me design and build a wheelchair that looked *very* cool—so that people would have an excuse to speak with me. I once saw a man in public riding around on a lazy-boy recliner that he had modified with a motor.

I would get a huge dog—a Great Dane—make a harness and have him pull me around. A dog like that would have people packing around. I would also train him to wear cool sunglasses (an elastic band would hold them on). I would have a really loud horn on the chair so that I could get people's attention. Once they looked, I would wave them over and give away tracts, which I would have in a special tract-rack that said, "Please take one."

I battle fear constantly, but I ignore it because of priorities. Firefighters battle fear, but they learn to ignore it because people's lives are at stake. Be like a firefighter . . . because people's eternities are at stake.

In July 2012, a lifeguard was fired from his Florida job because he left his zone to help rescue a nearby swimmer. This man was employed by an independent company whose policy instructed its lifeguards that if someone was drowning outside their prescribed area, they were to call 911. The 21-year-old ignored the policy and assisted in the rescue of the drowning man.[4]

Such a callous and senseless policy by the company reminded me of the religious leaders and their many objections to Jesus' healing on the Sabbath day. They rigidly kept the letter and ignored the spirit of the Law:

And he was teaching in one of the synagogues on the sabbath. And, behold, there was a woman which had a spirit of infirmity eighteen years, and was bowed together, and could in no wise lift up herself. And when Jesus saw her, he called her to him, and said unto her, Woman, thou art loosed from thine infirmity. And he laid his hands on her: and immediately she was made straight, and glorified God. And the ruler of the synagogue answered with indignation, because that Jesus had healed on the sabbath day, and said unto the people, There are six days in which men ought to work: in them therefore come and be healed, and not on the sabbath day. The Lord then answered him, and said, Thou hypocrite, doth not each one of you on the sabbath loose his ox or his ass from the stall, and lead him away to watering? And ought not this woman, being a daughter of Abraham, whom Satan hath bound, lo, these eighteen years, be loosed from this bond on the sabbath day? And when he had said these things, all his adversaries were ashamed: and all the people rejoiced for all the glorious things that were done by him (Luke 13:10-17, *KJV*).

Tragically, most Christians think evangelism is "out of their zone." They think the company policy is to have someone else do the task. But each of us is not just *called* to evangelize; we are *commanded* to go into the entire world and preach the gospel to every person (see Mark 16:15). The fact that we have had to be *commanded* to reach out to the lost reveals our wickedness. No one should have to be commanded to warn someone who is in terrible danger. We should therefore earnestly study how to present the gospel to a dying world, even if we feel overwhelmed by our present circumstances. This will not only please God, but it will lift us up above our Job experience and help us to see life in the perspective of eternity.

Some years ago a Christian brother who found himself in a very dark and painful Job experience began to write to me. He was slowly dying, and he asked for prayer. By trusting God and caring for others in this frightening situation, he was able to lift himself above his terminal cancer. This was one of his last emails to me:

I'm very thankful for Christ, for saving me and loving me so much. I praise God for His word, His every heartbeat and breath this body has had by His kindness. It's very early, and I'm happy to announce I'm not sad or afraid anymore. I don't feel much anymore, and I sleep about 18 hours a day. It's almost time . . . I don't know if I'll get to write you anymore . . . no regrets . . . just pray for my son who does not know Christ. I would've loved to have got to see him, but not God's will. I pray that you and *180* will change the world in the months to follow.

In Christ, Joe Wade[5]

Notice Joe's concern for other people's salvation. Love causes us to take our eyes off ourselves and look to the good of others. That's what the cross is all about. If you, like most of us, have trouble with fear, and that fear is stopping you from reaching out to the lost, don't ask God to release you from your fear. Instead, ask Him to fill you with love, because love will have the effect of overcoming your fears. Fear is a preoccupation with self, while love is occupied with the good of others.

What is it that gives Christians the courage and strength to minister to other people even when our hearts feel overwhelmed by our own grief and troubles? My friend Joe had a deep faith in God that reached through the veil of death and held onto the hand of Jesus. This attitude was evident in the life of Job, as well, in this second famous life-giving statement that he made:

For I know that my Redeemer lives, and He shall stand at last on the earth; and after my skin is destroyed, this I know, that in my flesh I shall see God, whom I shall see for myself, and my eyes shall behold, and not another. How my heart yearns within me! (Job 19:25-27).

Job, like my friend Joe, had complete assurance of salvation. Theodore Cuylar had this to say on the topic:

The secret sorrow which I dare not breathe to the most intimate friend—I can freely unbosom to my Savior. Ah, how well He knows every thorn which pricks my foot, and every wound which trickles its silent drops from my bleeding soul! This is a wondrous encouragement to prayer. For my

Physician will never administer the wrong medicine, nor fail to help us in the hour of sudden distress![6]

Perhaps you are a believer who needs to dig deeply into the truth of God's promise and gain courage from the assurance that He has redeemed you. If so, put your trust in God as you battle your hardships. Decide to take the message of "Life, life, eternal life!" to those who do not know Christ so that they too will begin to live with purpose and hope.

Perhaps as you read, however, you recognize that you have not experienced the new birth in Christ for yourself. Do you know God? Do you have the kind of intimacy with Him that Theodore Cuylar expressed? The Bible says, "Blessed are the dead who die in the Lord" (Rev. 14:13). Are you "in the Lord"? Can you say that you *know* that your Redeemer lives? Have you passed from death to life and thus received a faith that is an unshakeable certainty? If not, please put this book down, and plead for God to save you from your sins.

JOB AND SCIENTIFIC TRUTHS

Job 26:1-14; 28:25-28

If the Bible had only one scientific fact in its many pages that was proven true in our day, we could perhaps use the word "coincidence" to explain it. The verse could have been written by random chance. But the Scriptures have many such scientific facts recorded in them that weren't known to the world when they were written 3,000 years ago.

EARTH, CLOUDS AND THE OCEAN'S BOUNDARIES

We see a number of these scientific statements in the book of Job. For example, Job tells us, "He stretches out the north over empty space; He hangs the earth on nothing" (Job 26:7).

Job said that God hung the earth on nothing. But what he said was senseless in his day. The earth can't hang on *nothing*. A small stone can't hang on nothing, let alone this massive earth. Scientists estimate the earth's total weight by reckoning the weight of each of its parts: the crust (solid rock), the mantle (also solid rock), and the core. They have calculated that this comes to about 6.6 sextillion tons (that's 6,600,000,000,000,000,000,000 tons). But over time science has discovered the truth that was already revealed in the Bible: since the invisible force of gravity doesn't exist in space, this super heavy earth actually does hang on nothing. How could Job have known this? The only reasonable explanation is the one given in Scripture: "All Scripture is given by inspiration of God, and is profitable for doctrine, for reproof, for correction, for instruction in righteousness" (2 Tim. 3:16).

Back in the early 1700s, Matthew Henry wrote about this passage in Job that tells us that God hung the earth on nothing:

> If we look about us, to the earth and waters here below, we shall see striking instances of omnipotence, which we may gather out of these verses. (1.) *He hangs the earth upon nothing,* Job 26:7. The vast terraqueous globe neither rests upon any pillars nor hangs upon any axle-tree, and yet, by the almighty power of God, is firmly fixed in its place, poised with its own weight. The art of man could not hang a feather upon nothing, yet the divine wisdom hangs the whole earth so. It is *ponderibus librata suis—poised by its own weight,* so says the poet; it is *upheld by the word of God's power,* so says the apostle. What is hung upon nothing may serve us to set our feet on, and bear the weight of our bodies, but it will never serve us to set our hearts on, nor bear the weight of our souls.[1]

Job stated another fact unknown by the world in his day: "He binds up the water in His thick clouds, yet the clouds are not broken under it" (Job 26:8).

Clouds are made up of the liquid that evaporates from lakes, rivers, oceans and the hot human forehead. Heat from the sun causes this liquid to rise to a certain point in the sky, where it sits in the form of a cloud. One scientist simplified the weight of the clouds for kids by saying that a small cumulus cloud weighs about as much as 100 elephants. A thunderstorm cloud weighs more like 200,000 elephants. If you prefer pounds to elephants, a cloud that is about half a mile in width can weigh as much as 200,000 pounds, and a large cumulonimbus around two million pounds or more.

Even though clouds weigh hundreds of tons, they are in one sense weightless, even though they aren't in space. They remain within the confines of gravity, yet they defy gravity's pull. They "magically" become less dense than dry air of the same volume. Job was scientifically accurate in his statements. The water *is* bound in the thick clouds. It has a holding pattern, and it stays in the cloud until something triggers its release and causes it to return to the earth to water it and to give it life. Jesus told us who is in charge of the water department: "For He makes His sun rise on the evil and on the good, and sends rain on the just and on the unjust" (Matt. 5:45).

Job continued with another scientific truth: "He drew a circular horizon on the face of the waters, at the boundary of light and darkness" (Job 26:10). Matthew Henry commented on this verse:

> He sets bounds to the waters of the sea, and compasses them in (Job 26:10), that they may not return to cover the earth; and these bounds shall continue unmoved, unshaken, unworn, till the day and night come to an end, when time shall be no more. Herein appears the dominion which Providence has over the raging waters of the sea, and so it is an instance of his power, Jeremiah 5:22. We see too the care which Providence takes of the poor sinful inhabitants of the earth, who, though obnoxious to His justice and lying at His mercy, are thus preserved from being overwhelmed, as they were once by the waters of a flood, and will continue to be so, because they are reserved unto fire.[2]

Job finishes this portion of his thoughts about God by saying, "Indeed these are the mere edges of His ways, and how small a whisper we hear of Him!" (Job 26:14). How right he was.

GIVING CREDIT WHERE CREDIT IS DUE

Back in 2009 I took a camera crew to the evolution museum in Paris. Across the main entrance of the building are the words "Grand Gallery of Evolution, Natural History Museum." After about an hour of searching for displays on evolution, however, we asked an attendant to help us find one. The man directed us up some stairs, where we found a stuffed monkey in a glass case on which was written "Lucy." Yet the museum was filled with displays of stuffed giraffes, horses, elephants, fish, cows, lions, tigers, insects and fish—God's creation. The place looked like Noah's ark, and yet there wasn't a whisper of anything about God—the Creator of every animal. Humanity knows that God created all things, and yet so many of us refuse to give Him any praise. It is rather given to evolution as the creator. Here is how Paul explains it:

> For since the creation of the world His invisible attributes are clearly seen, being understood by the things that are made, even His eternal power and Godhead, so that they are without excuse, because, although they knew God, they did not glorify Him as God, nor were thankful, but became futile in their thoughts, and their foolish hearts were darkened (Rom. 1:20-21).

WINDS AND WATERS

Two chapters after making his first list, Job once again spoke to affirm the incredible ways of God:

> For He looks to the ends of the earth, and sees under the whole heavens, to establish a weight for the wind, and apportion the waters by measure. When He made a law for the rain, and a path for the thunderbolt, then He saw wisdom and declared it; He prepared it, indeed, He searched it out. And to man He said, "Behold, the fear of the Lord, that is wisdom, and to depart from evil is understanding" (Job 28:24-28).

God has established "a weight for the wind." Wind, invisible though it is, has both vertical and horizontal mass. Up until approximately 300 years ago, most believed that the air was empty and did not weigh anything. But we now know that wind has a vertical weight of 14.7 pounds per square inch. And if you do not believe that wind has a horizontal weight, you have never been in a hurricane or seen video of the wind throwing an 18-wheeler around as though it was a child's toy.

Job also informed us that God apportioned "the waters by measure." Did you know that there is no such thing as new water? While many things are genuinely "new" on the earth (you and I are among them; so are flowers, birds, trees and animals), every drop of water is as old as the day God created it. The Lord made a certain quantity of water and no more. He apportioned "the waters by measure."

Approximately 70 percent of the earth's surface is water covered, 96.5 percent of the water being in the oceans. The rest is in clouds, rivers, lakes, icecaps, glaciers, in the ground and in aquifers.[3] All this water is continually changing in form, thanks to the marvelous water cycle.

Our planet's water supply is constantly moving from one place to another and converting from one form to another. The natural water cycle (also known as the hydrologic cycle) describes the continuous movement of water on, above and below the surface of the earth. Most of us only notice the water that we see on the earth, but there are huge amounts of it in the ground—more than there is on the surface. Much of this underground water feeds our freshwater rivers. Rainfall continually resupplies this underground storage, and this stored water regularly recharges rivers through seepage.

Water is forever changing form from liquid to vapor to ice. Rain or snow or hail falls from the clouds, cleans the air on the way down, gives life to the earth, soaks into the soil, is under pressure (so that it will run uphill to push it above the ground surface), evaporates under the heat of the sun, rises to the clouds, and waits to go through the whole process once again. In the United States alone, we daily go through more than 300 billion gallons of surface water and more than 80 billion gallons of groundwater. As Job says, God gave us the water "by measure."

Historians tell us that the water cycle was discovered gradually over a period of many years. However, in the sixteenth century a scientist named Bernard Palissy compiled the theories and gave us our modern hydrological cycle.[4]

How could Job have known about these scientific truths 3,000 years ago except by divine inspiration?

JOB AND LUST

Job 31:1-4

As Job continued his discourse, he hit upon a topic that affects most of us on an ongoing basis: "I have made a covenant with my eyes; why then should I look upon a young woman?" (Job 31:1). Matthew Henry, whose outstanding commentary we have referred to several times, said this about Job 31:1-8:

> Job did not speak the things here recorded by way of boasting, but in answer to the charge of hypocrisy. He understood the spiritual nature of God's commandments, as reaching to the thoughts and intents of the heart. It is best to let our actions speak for us; but in some cases we owe it to ourselves and to the cause of God, solemnly to protest our innocence of the crimes of which we are falsely accused. The lusts of the flesh, and the love of the world, are two fatal rocks on which multitudes split; against these Job protests he was always careful to stand upon his guard.[1]

Job did have one advantage over those of us in today's Western society: he lived in a world in which a woman's shape was always covered. The Bible says that as Christians, we have escaped the corruption that is in the world through lust (see 2 Pet. 1:4), and lust certainly is "in the world" more than it ever has been in history. It's in our movies, on billboards, on the Internet, in magazines and in our music. It permeates this world. Lust is used to sell cars, booze, bread, horses, cats and dogs, because lust gets a man's attention.

But we should never think of the pleasures of lust without thinking of its constant bedfellow, death (see Jas. 1:15). The two go hand in hand. If you give yourself to lust, you give yourself to death, and death without the Savior's blood will damn you to Hell. Look at the warning of Holy Scripture:

> You have heard that it was said to those of old, "You shall not commit adultery." But I say to you that whoever looks at a woman to lust for her has already committed adultery with her in his heart. If your right eye causes you to sin, pluck it out and cast it from you; for it is more profitable for you that one of your members perish, than for your whole body to be cast into hell (Matt. 5:27-29).

We are further admonished:

> Do not love the world or the things in the world. If anyone loves the world, the love of the Father is not in him. For all that is in the world—the lust of the flesh, the lust of the eyes, and the pride of life—is not of the Father but is of the world. And the world is passing away, and the lust of it; but he who does the will of God abides forever (1 John 2:15-17).

WALKING ON WATER

With promiscuity so prevalent in society, we live on the edge of a raging ocean of lust that threatens to drown anyone who dares to swim in its shark-infested waters. As Christians, we are in the world but not of it. As we live here in this world, we often have to venture out into the ocean of temptation. So how does the Christian walk above this sea of lust? There are at least three keys.

Walk in the Spirit

In Galatians 5:16 Paul says, "Walk in the Spirit, and you shall not fulfill the lust of the flesh." This is a primary key to avoiding temptation and sin. Walking in the Spirit means to be mindful of the things of the Spirit of God. If you want to know what pleases the Holy Spirit, read the Word daily. Meditate on Scripture, and let its words renew your mind. And keep in mind that the Bible is no ordinary book. It is supernatural, from Genesis to Revelation. Its words are quick and powerful, sharper than any two-edged sword, and they go right into the marrow of the bones (see Heb. 4:12). Fill your mind with its supernatural truths. Cram the garden of your heart with beautiful flowers, and there will be no room for ugly weeds.

Cultivate the Fear of God

We have talked about this already, but cultivating the fear of God is vital if we want to avoid sin, including the sin of lust. The way to develop a healthy fear of God is to simply think the way that Job thought. In order to get a glimpse of the Creator and to understand Him, Job meditated on God's creation. As soon as Job spoke of lightning, he spoke of the fear of the Lord:

> When He made a law for the rain, and a path for the thunderbolt, then He saw wisdom and declared it; He prepared it, indeed, He searched it out. And to man He said, "Behold, the fear of the Lord, that is wisdom, and to depart from evil is understanding" (Job 28:26-28).

Think about lightning for a moment, and think about it with the lightning-Maker in mind. The air within a lightning bolt can heat up to 54,000 degrees Fahrenheit. In an instant it becomes six times hotter than the surface of the sun. A leader of a bolt of lightning—an ionized channel that creates a path for the lightning to travel along—can travel at speeds of 140,000 miles per hour. Now try to shake your mind free from the darkened understanding that clouds our unregenerate mind, and ask yourself what kind of Being could create the terrifying force of lightning? What sort of Being could conceive of it and then speak it into existence in the first place?

Such thoughts tend to produce a little of the fear of the Lord. Recognizing the power and the energy of God will help us to realize who we are sinning against—and justly angering—when we commit adultery in our heart by giving ourselves to lust. Those who don't fear God have a deficiency of understanding. They are like a baby who doesn't fear a thing. If you set a crawling infant near a thousand-foot cliff, he will crawl off the edge and fall to his death. He doesn't have fear, because he lacks knowledge. Once the baby gains a knowledge of gravity and heights (often painfully), he or she will wisely back away from dangerous situations.

Our fear of God shouldn't come only from the knowledge that we have sinned. We should fear God because He *is* to be feared. Angels stand in awe of Him, and demons tremble because of His infinite power. Jesus, in His humanity, gave us an example of what it means to walk in the fear of God (see Isa. 11:2). The Bible says of Jesus that "He was heard because of His godly fear" (Heb. 5:7).

To help us maintain the fear of God, our Creator has given us two (often overlooked) weapons against lust. They are our eyelids, and they can help us deal with lust with some quick shuteye. If you can't close your eyes for some reason, then turn your head. Look away from temptation, and plead with God to give you the strength not to play the hypocrite.

> For why should you, my son, be enraptured by an immoral woman, and be embraced in the arms of a seductress? For the ways of man are before the eyes of the LORD, and He ponders all his paths. His own iniquities entrap the wicked man, and he is caught in the cords of his sin. He shall die for lack of instruction, and in the greatness of his folly he shall go astray (Prov. 5:20-23).

Memorizing the Ten Commandments will also help us to fear the Lord and avoid sinning against Him. As you learn the commandments, keep in mind the spiritual nature of the Law—that God sees the thought life. God gave us the Law as a light to show us the subtle nature of sin:

> For the commandment is a lamp; and the law is light; and reproofs of instruction are the way of life: to keep thee from

the evil woman, from the flattery of the tongue of a strange woman. Lust not after her beauty in thine heart; neither let her take thee with her eyelids (Prov. 6:23-25, *KJV*).

Meditate on the Cross

Think about what the Son of God endured to set you free from sin. His flesh was ripped apart, His precious blood was shed, and His soul endured unspeakable suffering so that we could avoid the damnation of Hell. Every time we sin, we despise that sacrifice.

For most of us, the battle against sin is a daily and ongoing one. But in Jesus Christ we have already won the war. We know this through the prophecies that we find in Holy Scripture. So never for a moment surrender to the losing side. Stand fast in the liberty with which Christ has made us free.

In the next chapter we will see from Job's final words how we can further walk in victory.

JOB AND "IF"

Job 31:5-40

If you are wise, you will regularly check your flesh for something called melanomas. These are usually small and ugly growths on the flesh that can develop into deadly cancer. If you find a melanoma, you should quickly have it removed by a surgeon, and in doing so you may save your life.

It's wise for us to search our fleshly hearts, as well, for that which is cancerous and ugly in the sight of a holy God. As we do, we can save ourselves from great pain. Job 31 contains a mirror that can help us see areas of our lives that the eye may not normally be able to see. So with a searching eye and a tender conscience, we can say with the psalmist, "Search me, O God, and know my heart; try me, and know my anxieties; and see if there is any wicked way in me, and lead me in the way everlasting" (Ps. 139:23-24).

Job, as he neared the climax of his impassioned discourse, used the word "if" 19 times in chapter 31, saying, "If I have done a certain thing or failed to do something and have therefore sinned, let me be punished." We will ask the same questions of ourselves that Job contemplated, and if any sin is uncovered in our hearts, we can quickly flee to the blood of the One who was punished in our place and can be cleansed in an instant (see 1 John 1:9).

1. "If I have walked with falsehood . . ." (Job 31: 5)

King David said, "Behold, the wicked brings forth iniquity; yes, he conceives trouble and brings forth falsehood" (Ps. 7:14). David likened deceitful words to the fruit of pregnancy. Our love affair with sin naturally gives birth to lying lips. No one has to teach children to lie; each of us is born with the tendency to be crafty. But as people mature in life and become more sophisticated in their lying, it becomes clear that there is a seed planted within us that caused our deceitful condition. Those who lie have one thing in common: they are idolaters. They lie because they don't fear God, and they don't fear God because their perception of Him is flawed.

We can guard ourselves against the sin of idolatry—of a faulty view of God—in the same way we guard against all wrongdoing: by a thorough knowledge of the Scriptures. Meditate on portions of Scripture, such as Psalm 50:

> But to the wicked God says: "What right have you to declare My statutes, or take My covenant in your mouth, seeing you hate instruction and cast My words behind you? When you saw a thief, you consented with him, and have been a partaker with adulterers. You give your mouth to evil, and your tongue frames deceit. You sit and speak against your brother; you slander your own mother's son. These things you have done, and I kept silent; you thought that I was altogether like you; but I will rebuke you, and set them in order before your eyes.
>
> Now consider this, you who forget God, lest I tear you in pieces, and there be none to deliver: whoever offers praise glorifies Me; and to him who orders his conduct aright I will show the salvation of God" (Ps. 50:16-23).

It isn't easy for those with sinful hearts to snuggle up to the God who warns, "Lest I tear you in pieces." Passages like this will help us to quickly drop any flawed perspectives we have of the Lord.

2. "If my foot has hastened to deceit . . ." (Job 31:5)

Even after we come to faith in Christ, we have a propensity to sin. Our flesh hastens to the deceit of sin. The Scriptures warn us not to turn aside to sin's enticing voice: "But exhort one another daily, while it is called 'Today'; lest any of you be hardened through the deceitfulness of sin" (Heb. 3:13). It's healthy for us to have a fear of our own Adamic heart, which is like a deceitful bow that shoots crookedly. It can't be trusted. It will whisper to us justification for lust, lying, adultery and theft. Our sinful heart is a Judas, and it will betray us with a kiss.

3. "If my step has turned from the way, or my heart walked after my eyes . . ." (Job 31:7)

In the previous chapter of this book, we saw that Job said, "I have made a covenant with my eyes; why then should I *look* upon a young woman?" (Job 31:1, emphasis added). The *King James Version* says, "Why then should I *think* upon a maid?" Other versions translate the Hebrew word for "look" and "think" as "gaze." The eyes are the windows to our thoughts. If we *look* lustfully, we will *think* lustfully. In other words, it will affect our heart. Jesus said, "Whoever *looks* at a woman to lust for her has already committed adultery with her *in his heart*" (Matt. 5:28, emphasis added). Adam Clarke says:

> I made a covenant with mine eyes . . . "I have cut" or divided "the covenant sacrifice with my eyes." My conscience and my eyes are the contracting parties; God is the Judge; and I am therefore bound not to look upon anything with a delighted or covetous eye, by which my conscience may be defiled, or my God dishonored.[1]

Our physical hearts may pump physical blood and give life to our physical flesh, but it's the *spiritual* heart of man that gives life to his fleshly and sinful nature. Upon our conversion to Christ, God gives us a heart transplant, because our old hearts are terminal.

4. "If any spot adheres to my hands . . ." (Job 31:7)

Scripture often likens sin to spots of leprosy (see 1 Tim. 6:14; 2 Pet. 3:14). Leprosy is a dreaded disease, because it is contagious, and its symptoms are horrific. It develops slowly (over a time period of 6 months to 40 years) and results in skin lesions and deformities, most often affecting the parts of the body that get cold most easily—the eyes, nose, earlobes, hands, feet and private parts. Those who were affected with this disease in Bible times were considered outcasts.[2] Think of the horror in those days, when there was no cure, of discovering a spot of leprosy on your hand, and think about how quickly people would have wanted it removed before it spread through their whole body. That should be our attitude toward sin. Jesus said, "And if your right hand causes you to sin, cut it off and cast it from you; for it is more profitable for you that one of your members perish, than for your whole body to be cast into hell" (Matt. 5:30).

5. "If my heart has been enticed by a woman . . ." (Job 31:9)

A woman's body is like a magnet to the eyes of sinful man. Those ladies who flaunt themselves with split shirts, low necklines and see-through clothing are guilty of causing men to stumble. The Scriptures speak of the fate of those who cause the godly to trip: "But if you cause one of these little ones who trusts in me to fall into sin, it would be better for you to be thrown into the sea with a large millstone hung around your neck" (Mark 9:42, *NLT*). At the same time, as we have already mentioned, a man is responsible for what he chooses to gaze upon. When a man encounters a woman who is immodestly dressed, his best defense is to close his eyes, look away or, if he is able, to leave hastily.

6. "If I have lurked at my neighbor's door . . ." (Job 31:9)

We should never "give place to the devil" (Eph. 4:27) nor make provision for the flesh. Those who are tempted by adultery should run from temptation, just as Joseph ran when Potiphar's lusty wife enticed him to sin against God. Don't lurk at sin's door, because, as it did with Cain, sin lies at the door. God warned Cain that sin desired him but that he should overcome it. God asked him, "Why are you angry? And why has your countenance fallen? If you do well, will you not be accepted? And if you do not do well, sin lies at the door. And its desire is for you, but you should rule over it" (Gen. 4:6-7). Tragically, the anger in Cain's heart became murder through his hands. So it is with any sin. It lies at the door, waiting for an opportunity to pounce in and consume us. Slam the door shut, and lock it.

7. "If I have despised the cause of my male or female servant . . ." (Job 31:13)

Job was a rich man, but he never let his life status lift him above those who were less fortunate than he was. Scriptures rails against those who oppress their employees: "Indeed the wages of the laborers who mowed your fields, which you kept back by fraud, cry out; and the cries of the reapers have reached the ears of the Lord of Sabaoth. You have lived on the earth in pleasure and luxury; you have fattened your hearts as in a day of slaughter. You have condemned, you have murdered the just; he does not resist you" (Jas. 5:4-6).

8. "If I have kept the poor from their desire, or caused the eyes of the widow to fail, or eaten my morsel by myself, so that the fatherless could not eat of it . . ." (Job 31:16-17)

James gives us very clear instruction about what genuine faith will entail:

My brethren, do not hold the faith of our Lord Jesus Christ, the Lord of glory, with partiality. For if there should come into your assembly a man with gold rings, in fine apparel, and there should also come in a poor man in filthy clothes, and you pay attention to the one wearing the fine clothes and say to him, "You sit here in a good place," and say to the poor man, "You stand there," or, "Sit here at my footstool," have you not shown partiality among yourselves, and become judges with evil thoughts? (Jas. 2:1-4).

9. "If I have seen anyone perish for lack of clothing, or any poor man without covering . . ." (Job 31:19)

Job made sure that people didn't perish for lack of covering, and while we too should be concerned for the poor, we should also be deeply concerned that any person would perish because of a lack of spiritual covering on Judgment Day. Do you have a concern for the lost? Do you think of the fate of the ungodly? Does it burden you that if those who do not know Christ pass from this life in their sins, they will pass into the fire of God's wrath?

> Enter into the rock, and hide in the dust, from the terror of the LORD and the glory of His majesty. . . . They shall go into the holes of the rocks, and into the caves of the earth, from the terror of the LORD and the glory of His majesty, when He arises to shake the earth mightily (Isa. 2:10,19).

> It is a righteous thing with God to repay with tribulation those who trouble you, and to give you who are troubled rest with us when the Lord Jesus is revealed from heaven with His mighty angels, in flaming fire taking vengeance on those who do not know God, and on those who do not obey the gospel of our Lord Jesus Christ (2 Thess. 1:6-8).

Are you able to say with the apostle Paul, "*Knowing*, therefore, the terror of the Lord, we persuade men" (2 Cor. 5:11, emphasis added). Do you and I live to persuade men and women to flee to the cross for the mercy of God in Christ?

10. "If his heart has not blessed me, and if he was not warmed with the fleece of my sheep . . ." (Job 31:20)

Regeneration produces a power in our lives that enables us to shine brightly through our good works. Jesus said, "Let your light so shine before men, that they may see your good works and glorify your Father in heaven" (Matt. 5:16). We are here to benefit this world, not to fleece them as so many do in the name of Christianity. It takes energy to produce light, but in light of eternity, we must do so.

11. "If I have raised my hand against the fatherless, when I saw I had help in the gate . . ." (Job 31:21)

Scripture reminds us that "pure and undefiled religion before God and the Father is this: to visit orphans and widows in their trouble, and to keep oneself unspotted from the world" (Jas. 1:27).

12. "If I have made gold my hope, or said to fine gold, 'You are my confidence' . . ." (Job 31:24)

How easy it is to put our trust in money. This is why it's so difficult for the rich to enter Heaven. Those who have wealth *trust* in money for their food, clothing and health. Money can give us peace and joy, and it gives many a sense of security for the future. But it can also take the place that God should have in our lives, because it can fill our thoughts and hold our affections. The Bible says that we either serve God or money—we cannot serve both (see Luke 16:13).

13. "If I have rejoiced because my wealth was great, and because my hand had gained much . . ." (Job 31:25)

The sin of pride isn't confined to the rich. We can be proud of our humility, our ability to pray, sing or preach, or our rich knowledge of the Scriptures. But whatever we possess in this life only comes to us because of the ability that God gives us.

14. If I have observed the sun when it shines, or the moon moving in brightness, so that my heart has been secretly enticed, and my mouth has kissed my hand . . ." (Job 31:26-27)

There is something more subtle that pride. It isn't something we can see the way we can see a proud look. This characteristic does not display itself obviously in the way models, like peacocks, strut the latest fashions in New York or Paris. It is a *hidden* self-importance—a vanity called conceit. The word "conceit" gives a clue as to this quality's subtlety. Conceit *conceals* itself, and it takes a tender conscience for a person to even realize its poisonous presence in his life. A person who is conceited is wise in his own eyes, and he has a secretly high opinion of himself. He's like an obese person sneaking into the darkness of a closet and secretly devouring a large box of chocolates—consumed with his own interests but wanting no one to realize it. Sweet though self-indulgence may be to his taste, he's only harming himself.

15. "If I have rejoiced at the destruction of him who hated me, or lifted myself up when evil found him . . ." (Job 31:29)

We may say that we love those who hate us. But one test of our love is to see how we react when our enemies are struck down by adversity. If we rejoice at their distress, it shows that the love we have for them is superficial. We are merely paying lip service to the Word of God. Jesus said, "But I say to you who hear: Love your enemies, do good to those who hate you, bless those who curse you, and pray for those who spitefully use you" (Luke 6:27-28).

If someone hates me, I usually send them a fruit basket—for no apparent reason—and I include a card saying something like, "Thinking of you. I hope you enjoy this. Best wishes." If I detect a resentful attitude in an atheist, or if I encounter someone who is indignant toward me, then if the person will let me, I buy him lunch. I have seen many hateful attitudes softened greatly by genuine acts of kindness.

16. "If the men of my tent have not said, 'Who is there that has not been satisfied with his meat?' . . ." (Job 31:31)

Make sure that you financially take care of those who labor in your local church: "Let the elders who rule well be counted worthy of double honor, especially those who labor in the word and doctrine. For the Scripture says, 'You shall not muzzle an ox while it treads out the grain,' and, 'The laborer is worthy of his wages'" (1 Tim. 5:17-18).

17. "If I have covered my transgressions as Adam, by hiding my iniquity in my bosom, because I feared the great multitude, and dreaded the contempt of families, so that I kept silence and did not go out of the door . . ." (Job 31:33-34)

Be transparent with God. Don't be like Adam, who hid from God because of his sin. There's no place for us to hide, so immediately come out into the open with any transgressions, and let the blood of Christ cleanse you.

18. "If my land cries out against me, and its furrows weep together . . ." (Job 31:38)

Jesus said that the field of this world is white unto harvest. It will cry out against us if we ignore the labor to which we have been called. Paul spoke of his moral obligation by requesting prayer that he would open his mouth and speak as he "ought" to (see Col. 4:4). He said, "Woe is me if I do not preach the gospel!" (1 Cor. 9:16).

19. "If I have eaten its fruit without money, or caused its owners to lose their lives . . ." (Job 31:39)

God forgive us if we have ever indulged ourselves in the blessings of God. We must never be like the rich man who clothed himself in fine linen and ignored poor Lazarus at his gate (see Luke 16:19-21). Sinners lie at the gate of the Church—we must compel them to come in.

Job had poured out his pain, his questions and his defense. At this point the Scriptures tell us, "The words of Job are ended" (Job 31:40). It was finally time for God to speak.

JOB AND WATER

Job 38:1-11

Job had made quite a lengthy statement, and in it he had said some rather bold things. He had also appealed for an audience with the Lord. Now, without the accompaniment of angelic hosts or the sound of blasting trumpets, the Almighty God of creation broke through the silence of the heavens to speak to one man:

> Who is this who darkens counsel by words without knowledge? Now prepare yourself like a man; I will question you, and you shall answer Me.
>
> Where were you when I laid the foundations of the earth? Tell Me, if you have understanding. Who determined its measurements? Surely you know! Or who stretched the line upon it? To what were its foundations fastened? Or who laid its cornerstone, when the morning stars sang together, and all the sons of God shouted for joy?
>
> Or who shut in the sea with doors, when it burst forth and issued from the womb; when I made the clouds its garment, and thick darkness its swaddling band; when I fixed My limit for it, and set bars and doors; when I said, "This far you may come, but no farther, and here your proud waves must stop!" (Job 38:2-11).

Job was finally receiving an answer to his prayers! He had pleaded that God would give him an audience and answer the question as to why he was suffering. Now the invisible Creator of the universe, whom no man has seen nor can see—the One who spoke everything into existence—spoke to one meager man. And how did their conversation begin? It began with a divine rebuke: "Who is this who darkens counsel by words without knowledge?" Job's thoughts had been wrong. God told Job to pull himself together and be a man, and He told him that He had some questions—there would be 70, in fact—that He wanted Job to answer.

God's first question came with a little sanctified sarcasm and some divine anthropomorphism. Everyone knows that when you build a house, you must first predetermine the size of the structure and lay a level foundation. God asked Job where he had been when God had done this for the earth. Job hadn't existed, of course, when the voice of the eternal Creator had taken nothing and made it into the something upon which we now live, and he certainly didn't know how the Supernatural had done the impossible.

Neither had Job been around when God had "shut in the sea with doors, when it burst forth and issued from the womb." He had not existed when the Creator had "made the clouds its garment, and thick darkness its swaddling band" or when God had fixed the limit for the sea "and set bars and doors" or when God had said to the seas, "This far you may come, but no farther, and here your proud waves must stop!"

Where was the Lord going with all these questions that had obvious answers? Job had been longing to understand the reason for the terrible afflictions that had come upon him, but God did not give him any explanation for the misery he had undergone. God wanted Job to see beyond the reason for his suffering—to see himself in the light of God's greatness and His sovereign purpose for humanity.

We don't think too deeply about the fact that boundaries have been set for the oceans until an earthquake causes more than a tempest in a teapot. When a quake forces the water past its God-given boundaries, waves suddenly destroy cities and take lives. But boundaries there are. Even though we live on a massive ball that is covered by water, none of the water falls off the "bottom." Water, hanging upside-down, as it were, clings to the earth as does a flea to a mangy dog. But it gets even stranger. Another God-created ball that sits in space 238,900 miles away from the earth invisibly pulls the oceans back and forth in what we call tides. Each and every day there are two high tides and two low tides. The time between high and low tide is just over six hours, so the complete tidal cycle repeats itself four times each day. The symmetry of the tides parallels the regular orbit of the moon around the earth and the rotation of the earth as it orbits around the sun.

While the bone-dry moon pulls the oceans on the earth, modern science doesn't know how on earth all this water got here on earth:

> Moon rocks collected by Apollo astronauts 40 years ago contain evidence that the moon's interior is bone dry, contrary to some more recent reports, say researchers. The conclusion is based on a new study focusing on chlorine isotopes in moon rocks, which are quite different from those found in terrestrial minerals. The discovery could be a step towards solving the riddle of where Earth's water came from.[1]

There's only a riddle if we close our eyes to the Scriptures. If a scientist, however, publically admits that he believes the Genesis account of creation, he brings with that declaration what is seen by the world as the intellectually bankrupt baggage of Adam and Eve, Noah's flood, Jonah and the great fish, and other biblical accounts, and not many scientists want that sort of humiliation among their academic peers. Besides, when the door to Genesis is closed, a door of endless conjecture opens, and that issues in a welcome breeze of relief from the stifling heat of moral accountability.

ROCKS WITH TAILS

But if God didn't make the water that gives the earth its life, how did it all get here? There have been a number of theories:

For a long time, astronomers thought that comets—chunks of ice and rock with tails of evaporating ice and with long, looping orbits around the Sun—were the likely culprit. However, remote measurements of the water evaporating off of several major existing comets (Halley, Hyakutake, and Hale-Bopp) revealed that their water ice was made of a different type of H_2O (containing a heavier isotope of hydrogen) than Earth's, suggesting that these comets could not be the source of our water.[2]

Some thoughtful person asked a learned scientist:

Is there a geophysical/chemical process that creates "new water" or is all water simply reprocessed previously existing water (i.e., evaporation, rain, etc.)? If the latter, this forces the question where did the original water come from? I heard on a TV show that some scientists think it came from meteors that crashed into the earth billions of years ago. But this forces the question, "How did water form on the meteors and why the same process couldn't have occurred on earth?"[3]

The expert replied:

All the water, or most of it, that is on the Earth today was here since the Earth cooled, around 4 billion years or so. When Earth was forming it was a molten mass but there is always water, in its molecular form. They formed clouds and then rain. Rain formed oceans and seas. The water condensed out again and the process continues to this day. It's called the "Water Cycle."

    I think the program you were watching was probably talking about molecular water. There is molecular water throughout the cosmos. There is even the signature of molecular water found in the chromatograph analysis of stellar light from the center of our galaxy. So it stands to reason that you can find some on meteors and asteroids. Also, meteors are just chunks of broken planets. The same processes that went into making their parent planet may have been the same ones that created ours. So there would be molecular water trapped in them as well. When the Earth was forming it was bombarded with hoards of asteroids and meteors. All of them probably carried some molecular water which got incorporated into the body of our Earth. Remember that this is *not* liquid water as we know it. It is just a very stable molecule. When you get a lot of them together you get water as we think of it.

So it might be, probably is, a combination of processes that got the water here in the first place.[4]

So there you have it. All the water "probably" came to earth on meteors, and the water that was on them came from planets that were "probably" formed by meteors with water on them, and that process goes way back in time, each planet bringing forth after its own kind. There was neither rhyme nor reason. It just happened. Each planet that had the complex and fortunate water-structure of two parts hydrogen and one part oxygen for some reason exploded and sent meteors into space. These meteors then hit the waterless earth and fortunately had exactly the right amount of water to form the Pacific, Atlantic and other oceans and to form the 307 million lakes that we now have puddled on the planet.[5]

If water arrived on earth as salt water—which is what is in the oceans—how and why did some of it evolve into fresh water? It's fortunate indeed that some of it processed itself into fresh water, because salt water is a killer. If we drink it, the intake of salt sends the body into severe dehydration, possibly leading to seizures, unconsciousness and brain damage, overwhelming the kidneys and resulting in death.

It's also fortunate that Mother/Father Evolution thought of the complex water cycle so that the salt water could be purified and then fall back down onto the earth so that you and I could drink it and live.

Rather than blindly believing all this absurdity, however, we could solve the riddle by believing the sensibility of Genesis 1:2, which tells us that God created the water. Job, even as the Lord was rebuking him, was well aware of this truth, and his response of silent, humble acceptance is exactly what ours should be.

JOB AND THE WONDERS OF CREATION

Job 38:12-38

God continued to speak of His creation, and as He did so, He revealed *precise* scientific facts that wouldn't be discovered by humanity until thousands of years after He made these statements. Charles Spurgeon wrote of God's questioning of Job:

> JEHOVAH had spoken, Job had trembled. The Lord had revealed Himself, Job had seen Him. Truly, God did but display the skirts of His robe and unveil a part of His ways. But therein was so much of ineffable glory that Job laid his hand upon his mouth in token of his silent consent to the claims of the Everlasting One. God spoke to Job out of the whirlwind concerning the greatness of His power, the wonders of His workings, the splendor of His skill, the infinity of His wisdom. Carefully read that wonderful speech of the Most High to the trembling Patriarch. I dare not call it poetry. For it rises as much above human poetry as the most sublime poetry stands above the poorest prose.[1]

But before we look at these truths that no man had yet uncovered, let's not pass over God's words about the simple dawning of each day, because they provoke some interesting thoughts:

Have you commanded the morning since your days began, and caused the dawn to know its place, that it might
take hold of the ends of the earth, and the wicked be
shaken out of it? (Job 38:12-13).

Have you ever considered what is really happening each
morning as the rays of the rising sun burst onto your local horizon? Have you thought about the fact that the sun has actually
never risen? The sun stays still. It's the turn of the earth that
makes us think that the sun is rising.

While the sun is "rising" in our area, it is "setting" at exactly
the same moment somewhere else on the earth. While we are
welcoming the dawn, someone somewhere else is looking at the
same sun as it sets and is saying goodbye to another day. Every
minute of every day, somewhere on this earth the same sun is
setting and at the same moment rising. There's not a second of
any day that it is not rising and setting simultaneously somewhere on this planet.

While it is rising and setting, the sun is also in the middle of
the sky, burning down on the deserts of Africa and simultaneously providing barely any warmth over the skies of a wintery
Alaska. God is the One responsible for this mindboggling and
perfectly balanced process.

As we look at these scientific facts that God revealed to Job,
the implications of them are extremely profound. They prove, as
we have noted before, that the Bible is the Word of the omniscient Creator, which means that its claims are more than worthy
of serious investigation. As we mentioned earlier, it's a fact of life
that we are going to die. The reality is that death could seize on
you before you even finish this sentence.

Thankfully, that didn't happen (assuming you are still reading), but death could still come to any of us in the next minute
or tomorrow or the next day or month or year. We have no hope
of immortality outside of that revealed in the Bible, which has
proven its authenticity. The Bible's message is that God will reveal Himself to us and grant us the gift of everlasting life upon

our obedience to the gospel (see John 14:21; Eph. 2:8-9). Speaking of Jesus, the Bible tells us:

> In the days of his flesh, when he had offered up prayers and supplications with strong crying and tears unto him that was able to save him from death, [he] was heard in that he feared; though he were a Son, yet learned he obedience by the things which he suffered; and being made perfect, he became the author of eternal salvation unto all them that obey him (Heb. 5:7-9, *KJV*).

> And we are His witnesses to these things, and so is also the Holy Spirit whom God has given to those who obey Him (Acts 5:32).

We are not saved because we are obedient; rather, we are obedient because we are saved. We can't earn God's mercy through obedience, repentance or faith (see Eph. 2:8-9). Our obedience merely shows that we have a new heart that delights to do God's will.

Keep these thoughts in mind as we look at undeniable information that proves beyond a doubt that the Bible is the Word of God. Please examine the truths we consider without prejudice, and remember too that the Bible isn't a scientific book. If God had intended it to be so, He could have explained to Job the principles of flight and told him about jumbo jets, motor vehicles, radios, telephones, televisions and iPads. But He didn't. These scientific facts we are about to examine are icing on the cake of all that God is and has for us, and it's only a thin layer.

SPRINGS OF THE SEA

"Have you entered the springs of the sea? Or have you walked in search of the depths?" (Job 38:16). It's only in recent years that modern deep-sea cameras have been able to capture images of hot-water vents on the floor of the ocean, proving this Scripture to be true. These hot-water springs release massive amounts of water in the darkness of the ocean floor.

Scientists constructed special submarines that were able to withstand the three-tons-per-square-inch pressure exerted on the ocean floor. These underwater vehicles made it possible for them to see deep-sea springs on the bottom of the oceans. The first observation is said to have taken place on the Mid-Atlantic Ridge by Project FAMOUS back in 1973. Other scientists then discovered huge hot springs on the Galapagos Rift in the Pacific Ocean in a submarine called *Alvin* in 1977. The Galapagos Rift springs were described in detail in the November 1979 issue of *National Geographic*. The article was titled "Incredible World of the Deep-sea Rifts" and had the caption "Scientists explore rifts in the seafloor where hot springs spew minerals and startling life exists in a strange world without sun."[2]

The Hidden Treasures

"Have you entered the treasury of snow?" (Job 38:22). Back in 1590 two Dutch spectacle-makers put several lenses in a tube and discovered that an object when viewed through the tube looked larger than it actually was, and thus they invented the compound microscope. The renowned Galileo heard of their discovery and began to conduct experiments of his own. He added a device to focus the microscope he had made, creating the telescope.

These two inventions opened a whole new world that previously had been invisible to the human eye. However, God had spoken of this unseen world of snow 3,000 years before these inventions were conceived of. Through microscopes we discovered the amazing treasures of the snow. With them we were suddenly able to examine snow crystals and see that each one is a gem of delicate, lace-like symmetry. Each individual flake is a perfect hexagonal shape, yet each one has a different intricate design. W. A. Bentley of Jericho, Vermont, first photographed snowflakes in 1885, and he eventually made micro-photographs of 4,800 snow crystals, no two of which are alike. He said:

Under the microscope, I found that snowflakes were miracles of beauty; and it seemed a shame that this beauty should not be seen and appreciated by others. Every crystal was a masterpiece of design and no one design was ever repeated. When a snowflake melted, that design was forever lost. Just that much beauty was gone, without leaving any record behind.[3]

There are four basic snowflake shapes:

1. *Stellar dendrite snowflakes* are the most common. The word "stellar" means "star-like," and "dendrite" means "tree-like." These flakes have the appearance of stars that have tiny "branches."
2. *Hexagonal plate snowflakes* are very thin and are made of solid ice, looking like a dinner plate with six sides.
3. *Column snowflakes* are longer and thinner, looking similar to the columns found on buildings. Each column snowflake has six sides.
4. *Needle snowflakes* are extremely thin and long and look, as one would expect, very much like needles. These too have six sides.

DIFFUSED LIGHT

"By what way is light diffused, or the east wind scattered over the earth?" (Job 38:24). The Hebrew word that is translated "diffused" is *chalaq,* which means "separated." Light can be separated into seven colors of the spectrum: red, orange, yellow, green, blue, indigo and violet. It wasn't until 1666 that Sir Isaac Newton used a prism to diffuse a beam of light into bands.

Newton said, "There are more sure marks of authenticity in the Bible than in any profane history. . . . I have a fundamental belief in the Bible as the Word of God, written by men who were inspired. I study the Bible daily."

TALKING LIGHT

"Can you send out lightnings, that they may go, and say to you, 'Here we are!'?" (Job 38:35). God now asked Job something that seems to be ludicrous. He asked Job if he could send out lightning—lightning that would go out and then manifest itself in the form of speech. This Bible verse made no sense to people until scientists came to understand that lightning is the source of radio waves. NASA explains:

> The source of most VLF emissions [radio waves] on Earth is lightning.[4] Lightning strokes emit a broadband pulse of radio waves, just as they unleash a visible flash of light. VLF signals from nearby lightning, heard through the loudspeaker of a radio, sound like bacon frying on a griddle or the crackling of a hot campfire. . . . Radio waves can propagate such great distances by bouncing back and forth between our planet's surface and the ionosphere—a layer of the atmosphere ionized by solar ultraviolet radiation. "The ionosphere and the surface of the Earth form a natural waveguide for VLF signals," explains Bill Taylor, a space scientist at the Goddard Space Flight Center.[5]

Sound waves travel at the speed of sound (about 600 miles per hour). However, radio waves travel at the speed of light (186,000 miles per second), because they are actually light waves. This is why we can have instantaneous wireless communication (through a phone call) with someone on the other side of the earth. Science didn't discover this until 1864 when "British scientist James Clerk Maxwell suggested that electricity and light waves were two forms of the same thing" (Modern Century Illustrated Encyclopedia).

Again, the only way to reconcile in our minds the Bible maintaining that lightning goes forth and then manifests itself in the form of speech is to concede that this concept could only come from the infinite mind of our omniscient Creator. But these weren't the only astonishing truths that Job heard from the mouth of God.

JOB AND THE HOLOCAUST

Job 40:1-5

After speaking to Job about creation for some time, God began to talk to Job about his delusions of grandeur. The Lord asked him another very direct question: "Shall the one who contends with the Almighty correct Him? He who rebukes God, let him answer it" (Job 40:2).

Job had sunk to a point of setting himself in opposition to his Creator, attempting to correct Him and even to rebuke Him. Such talk isn't unusual for sinful humanity. While those who fear God shudder at the thought of someone rebuking Him, it is no big leap for a sinner who uses God's name in vain to stand in moral judgment over Him, to rebuke and correct the Lord for what that person perceives to be His moral shortcomings. Such imprudence can only come from the ignorant—from those who lack knowledge.

THE BIG QUESTION

Why does God allow people to suffer? Why does He not put a stop to things that cause us pain? That is the big question. We tend to take the blessings in our lives for granted and to think that we are entitled to an easy time of things. After all, if God is good, then He should treat us nicely all the time, right?

I had tears in my eyes as I read an auto-obituary of a man who had died of throat cancer. This is what was published in a local newspaper on the day he died:

I was a true Scientist. Electronics, chemistry, physics, auto mechanic, wood worker, artist, inventor, business man, ribald comedian, husband, brother, son, cat lover, cynic. I had a lot of fun. It was an honor for me to be friends with some truly great people. I thank you. I've had great joy living and playing with my dog, my cats and my parrot. But, the one special thing that made my spirit whole, is my long love and friendship with my remarkable wife, my beloved Mary Jane. I loved her more than I have words to express. Every moment spent with my Mary Jane was time spent wisely. Over time, I became one with her, inseparable, happy, fulfilled. I enjoyed one good life. Traveled to every place on earth that I ever wanted to go. Had every job that I wanted to have. Learned all that I wanted to learn. Fixed everything I wanted to fix. Eaten everything I wanted to eat. My life motto was: "Anything for a Laugh." Other mottos were "If you can break it, I can fix it," "Don't apply for a job, create one." I had three requirements for seeking a great job: 1—All glory, 2—Top pay, 3—No work. Now that I have gone to my reward, I have confessions and things I should now say. As it turns out, I *am* the guy who stole the safe from the Motor View Drive Inn back in June, 1971.[1]

This man went on to confess some of the things he had done in life that he knew were wrong and to say how he regretted smoking cigarettes, which were the cause of his untimely death. My tears were for his pain and suffering and for the anguish of his family. This man had lived a rich, happy and full life for which he was evidently thankful. But something was missing from his obituary—and it's something that most of us wouldn't even notice was missing.

God is the One who gave this man—and all of us—life. He created us and provided us with the ability to enjoy all kinds of wonderful blessings. So how then should we react to His kindness? We should love the Lord with all our heart, soul, mind and strength. That's the first and greatest commandment. We are to put God first in our affections, loving Him and being thankful to Him because of who He is and what He has done for us. But this man who had a wonderful life didn't even mention the One who had given him his many blessings, let alone thank Him.

Everything we touch, taste, see, feel or hear that brings us pleasure should be responded to with a heart of gratitude. Ungratefulness is a serious sin. If you don't think being thankless is a big deal, how do you react when someone is ungrateful to you? If we do someone a favor, we naturally think that the least that person can do is be thankful and show some appreciation. How much more then should every one of us give a humble and heartfelt thanks to God for giving us life itself? To love God with all our heart, mind, soul and strength is simply to do what is right. But humanity is so willfully blind, unabashedly selfish and unspeakably ungrateful that such a thought doesn't even enter our godless minds. We snatch the Lord's blessings directly from the hand of God, and we give gratitude and praise to nature, evolution or ourselves. God is ignored, and His name is despised and blasphemed. On top of that, we wrongly assume that when we die we are going to our reward, as if God is obligated to eternally care for us.

A friend once wrote to me and said that after he had shared the gospel in public, he noticed an elderly man in a wheelchair and decided to speak with him. But when he approached the man, my friend found that he was very angry. This man yelled, "Where was your good God when I was in the concentration camp? Was He on paid vacation when I saw my children being burnt alive?" My friend tried to speak with the distraught man, but the man was so angry that my friend wasn't able to get a word in. It was a difficult situation in which to answer such a sensitive question.

Why did God not intervene and stop the deaths of this man's beloved children? Why does He not intervene in the suffering that any of us goes through? One can't imagine the agony of horror that this concentration camp survivor went through. Since this

poor man had never found an answer, we can easily sympathize
with his bitterness and anger toward God. But let's pull back from
the immediacy of our suffering and look at some truths that are
relevant to this profound question.

THE BIGGER PICTURE

Every day, somewhere in this world, we can be sure that children are
being sexually molested, raped, beaten, prostituted and even murdered, and it seems that in almost all those cases, God doesn't intervene. He has let approximately 60 million babies die through legalized
American abortion. Every 24 hours thousands of children die of
starvation, and God doesn't do anything. Children this very day will
die of cancer and leave grieving parents with nothing but empty
grief and unanswered questions as to why God didn't help their
beloved child. In the near future we can know that thousands of
children will drown in water, be crushed in car accidents and die in
tornadoes, hurricanes and earthquakes—all while God looks on.

We surmise that if God is good, He is morally obligated do
something to stop this terrible suffering. When He doesn't do what
we think He should, we wrongly conclude that He is either heartless or evil.

What we see in real life is consistent with what we see of the
God revealed in Holy Scripture: God allows children and adults to
die today, and we see that happening in the Bible as well. But the
Scriptures go even further. In the Bible we read that God *caused* the
deaths of men, women and children in Noah's flood (see Gen. 6:5-
7). He *told* Joshua to kill every Canaanite man, woman and child
without mercy (see Deut. 20:16-17, for example). Scripture doesn't
hide the justice of God. It lays it bare:

> The fear of the LORD is clean, enduring forever; the judgments
> of the LORD are true and righteous altogether (Ps. 19:9).

> And I heard another from the altar saying, "Even so, Lord
> God Almighty, true and righteous are Your judgments"
> (Rev. 16:7).

God is holy, and to do what is right and just, He should damn the human race to Hell because of our wickedness. His goodness calls for His wrath. But His love calls for His mercy—which is why Jesus suffered God's wrath for us. If God wasn't the essence of love and mercy, we would *all* be in Hell right now. He *allows* suffering and evil to take place, but He promises to one day stop both suffering and evil.

Remember, God didn't intervene when John the Baptist was murdered, when James was killed with a sword, or when the eleven disciples were murdered for their faith. He didn't intervene when down through the ages the Roman Catholic Church martyred multitudes. He didn't intervene, and yet He remains sinless, without guilt, because all His judgments are righteous and true altogether.

Perhaps you don't believe that God is like that. You believe that He is good, kind and loving; that He's not the wrath-filled God of holiness as revealed in Scripture. But if you reject the biblical revelation of God, you will be left with a worse dilemma. The God you envision, the one who does not hold people accountable, will still allow children to be sexually molested, raped, beaten, prostituted, murdered and to die of starvation and cancer—but He will not do anything to help them, as He does in the Scripture. So your idea of God isn't loving or kind. An unbiblical God, whom you believe in, is heartless and doesn't believe in ultimate justice. But any judge who lets criminals go unpunished isn't good; he's evil and should be prosecuted himself. If he's good, a judge must see that justice is done. But your idea of a God who does not punish sinners leads to the conclusion that He couldn't care less that Hitler killed six million Jews. On top of that, this view of God offers you no hope of deliverance from suffering and death.

THE DIFFERENCE

When the moral Law and the justice of God enter the equation, they bring light to this incomprehensible question of God's inaction. It shows us that our righteously indignant demand for divine action is misguided. God is not to be blamed for the suffering of this world, because *we* are the guilty party. The Law shows us that we are ungrateful, unthankful, sin-loving, self-righteous, blasphemous and vile sinners, and we are pointing a holier-than-thou and judgmental finger at our morally perfect Creator.

Job responded to God's question appropriately. He didn't try to justify himself or continue to accuse God of wrongdoing. Instead, he humbled himself and said, "Behold, I am vile; what shall I answer You? I lay my hand over my mouth. Once I have spoken, but I will not answer; yes, twice, but I will proceed no further" (Job 40:4-5).

JOB AND THE DINOSAUR

Job 40:15-24

The Lord was not finished with Job. Again, God pointed to the marvels of creation, especially to the largest of the many creatures He had created:

> Behold now behemoth, which I made with thee; he eateth grass as an ox. Lo now, his strength is in his loins, and his force is in the navel of his belly. He moveth his tail like a cedar: the sinews of his stones are wrapped together. His bones are as strong pieces of brass; his bones are like bars of iron. He is the chief of the ways of God: he that made him can make his sword to approach unto him (Job 40:15-19, *KJV*).

A number of Bible commentators have theorized that the behemoth may have been a hippopotamus or an elephant. But neither of these fit its description, because the Scriptures tell us that the behemoth had a tail like a massive tree. A hippo's tail looks more like a twig than a tree, and the elephant's tail looks rather like a frayed piece of rope.

I believe (as do many others) that Scripture is talking about the dinosaur. This is what these five verses (written around 2,000 years BC) tell us about this animal:

1. "He eateth grass as an ox" (40:15). This creature was herbivorous (plant-eating). According to one article, "Although paleontologists claim to have found bigger dinosaurs, Argentinosaurus is the biggest sauropod whose size has been backed up by convincing evidence.[1] *This gigantic plant-muncher* . . . measured about 120 feet from head to tail and may have weighed over 100 tons" (emphasis added).[2]

Illustration by Nobu Tamura. Used by permission under the GNU Free Documentation License.

2. "His strength is in his loins, and his force is in the navel of his belly" (40:16). The *World English Bible* translates the verse, "Look now, his strength is in his thighs, his force is in the muscles of his belly." According to *Science Daily,* a new dinosaur named *Brontomerus mcintoshi*, or "thunder-thighs" after its enormously powerful thigh muscles, has been discovered in Utah.[3]

3. "He moveth his tail like a cedar" (40:17). This creature had a tail that moved like a large tree. "Western red-cedars of the Pacific Northwest are some of the most massive of the world's trees. . . . The biggest known specimens—on Washington's Olympic Peninsula and Vancouver Island—approach 20 feet across."[4]

4. "His bones are as strong pieces of brass; his bones are like bars of iron" (40:18). Clearly, any creature of this

size and weight must have had very strong bones: "120 tons [is] the weight of one Argentinosaurus, the heaviest of all animals, equal to 100 elephants."[5]

5. "He is the chief of the ways of God" (40:19). While a few modern versions translate the Hebrew word *re'shiyth* as "first" and not "chief," both words convey a specific contextual meaning.

According to theologian Dave Miller, "We are forced to conclude that when God referred to behemoth as the 'first' or 'chief' of His ways, He was referring primarily, if not exclusively, to its size and strength. . . . This conclusion is further supported by behemoth's specific features that God brings to Job's attention—features that inherently imply size, mass, weight, bulk, and strength: 'his strength is in his hips' (v. 16), 'his power is in his stomach muscles' (v. 16), 'he moves his tail like a cedar' (v. 17), 'his bones are like beams of bronze' (v. 18), 'his ribs like bars of iron' (v. 18)."[6]

There are some who contend that the dinosaur isn't as large as the blue whale, which proves that the words of Job 40 are erroneous. The longest whale ever discovered, however, measured in at just over 110 feet, and a recent discovery found that a dinosaur was more than 35 feet longer than the biggest whale. This "supersaurus" was one of the longest land animals ever found. It was a long-necked, whip-tailed giant measuring about 138 feet.[7]

6. "He that made him can make his sword to approach unto him" (40:19). The Wycliffe translation says, "He, who made him, shall set his sword against him." What was it that caused the dinosaurs to disappear? There are many theories. According to a news report back on May 10, 2001, "From new fossil evidence, scientists say they now know a mass extinction that preceded the age

of large dinosaurs happened relatively fast—perhaps when an asteroid crashed to Earth."[8]

Then on October 31, 2006, it was reported: "New evidences suggest that the global mass extinction at the end of the Dinosaur Era might not have been produced by the single Chicxulub meteor impact, found in Yucatan peninsula (Southern Mexico), but by multiple meteor impacts, massive volcanism in India, and climate changes."[9] On May 7, 2012, we were informed, "Dinosaurs 'gassed' themselves into extinction, British scientists say. The researchers calculated that the prehistoric beasts pumped out more than 520 million tons of methane a year—enough to warm the planet and hasten their own eventual demise."[10] While learned scientists play their "perhaps" and "may" guessing game, the Bible tells us why there are no living dinosaurs on the earth. The God who made them caused their sword to approach them. He caused their extinction.

A. Behemoth ate grass. So did the dinosaur.
B. Its strength was in its hips. So was the dinosaur's.
C. It had a tail like a large tree. So did the dinosaur.
D. It had very strong bones. So did the dinosaur.
E. It was the largest creature ever made. So was the dinosaur.
F. It became extinct. So did the dinosaur.

In His questioning of Job, God was actually communicating much to him. Job listened to this sobering list of 70 questions, and he quickly recognized that even the grievous, unexplainable suffering he'd had to endure gave him no excuse for questioning the almighty God.

JOB AND THE FUTURE

Job 42:1-6

Job had received his much-wanted personal encounter with God. It was now his turn to speak. What did Job have to say to the Lord?

> Then Job answered the Lord and said: "I know that You can do everything, and that no purpose of Yours can be withheld from You. You asked, 'Who is this who hides counsel without knowledge?' Therefore I have uttered what I did not understand, things too wonderful for me, which I did not know. Listen, please, and let me speak; You said, 'I will question you, and you shall answer Me.' I have heard of You by the hearing of the ear, but now my eye sees You. Therefore I abhor myself, and repent in dust and ashes" (Job 42:1-6).

Job now experientially understood that nothing is impossible with God. God can do anything. He sees all, and He even knows the future. He is the One who created the dimension of time, and even that is at His beck and call.

It is safe to say that only God knows the future. Some may believe that Satan has foreknowledge, but people may think that Satan knows the future simply because he believes the Scriptures to the point of trembling. The devil knows that if the Word of God says something, it will certainly come to pass. In speaking of the demonic realm, the Bible says:

But rather what we are setting forth is a wisdom of God once hidden [from the human understanding] and now revealed to us by God—[that wisdom] which God devised and decreed before the ages for our glorification [to lift us into the glory of His presence]. *None of the rulers of this age or world perceived and recognized and understood this, for if they had, they would never have crucified the Lord of glory* (1 Cor. 2:7-8, *AMP*, emphasis added).

C. S. Lewis said, "There is no uncreated being except God. God has no opposite. . . . The proper question is whether I believe in devils. I do. That is to say, I believe in angels, and I believe that some of these, by the abuse of their free will, have become enemies to God. . . . Satan, the leader or dictator of devils, is the opposite, not of God, but of Michael."[1]

NOSTRADAMUS AND OTHERS

If any human being knew what was going to happen in the next 10 minutes, or even in the next 2 minutes, he or she would move to Las Vegas and become a billionaire. But the truth is that no one knows what card will turn up next or how the dice will fall. Weathermen sometimes get the future right because of a calculated guess based on past and present knowledge, but many a parade has been rained upon because the weatherman really didn't know what would happen the next day.

There is a big difference between the apparent prophecies of Nostradamus and other professed seers and the prophecies of the Bible. Nostradamus's readers understand his predictions in retrospect—that is, after the supposed event has occurred. They are nebulous and mystical. Nostradamus wrote a thousand quatrains about what he thought were future events, and some of these events do seem to have been fulfilled. But if a person fires a thousand arrows into the air, some will come down and hit a target somewhere. Something else to note is that at the time Nostradamus wrote his quatrains, the Roman Catholic

Church forbade the reading of the Bible, but Nostradamus read the Scriptures in secret. This is why he wrote of a coming anti-Christ, earthquakes and "rumors of wars" (Matt. 24:6).

These are biblical terms, so it is obvious that Nostradamus took some of his prophecies from the Bible. Anyone who is ignorant of Bible prophecies will be impressed with some of the predictions of Nostradamus, believing that they were his own when in fact they were not. The Bible, on the other hand, is extremely specific in the way it details future events about the time when each prophecy's fulfillment would take place. The prophecies of Scripture were never intended to be interpreted in retrospect.

Those who are fans of Nostradamus may feel a sense of fascination as they try to piece together the puzzles of his quatrains. But in the end, there's no agenda in his words. There is no conclusion or direction. The prophecies of the Bible, however, have an agenda. Even though the Bible is a collection of 66 books written by 40 people over a period of 1,500 years, the Scriptures have one thread of continuity: In the Old Testament God promised to destroy man's greatest enemy, death. In the New Testament, we see how He did it.

God used certain men to pen His letter to humanity, and prophecy shows His fingerprints all over the Bible. I've been a Christian for more than 40 years, and there has never been a day in those 40 years that I haven't read the Bible. I can testify that it stands head, shoulders and body above every other "holy book," because those other books lack the prophetic seal.

THE SIGNS OF THE TIMES

Again, the Scriptures are filled with *precise* prophecies, written thousands of years ago about events that would take place in the future. So if details about the dinosaur weren't big enough evidence for you, look no further. Here are the signs of the times in which we live—God's long ago foretelling of a future that is unfolding today.

False Bible Teachers

The Bible speaks of false Bible expositors who will come in the last days—a perfect synopsis of today's televangelist with his promise of wealth and his bottomless collection bag. The Scripture says that these Bible teachers will be smooth, money-hungry talkers, will have many followers and will slur the Christian faith:

> But there were also false prophets among the people, even as there will be false teachers among you, who will secretly bring in destructive heresies, even denying the Lord who bought them, and bring on themselves swift destruction. And many will follow their destructive ways, because of whom the way of truth will be blasphemed. By covetousness they will exploit you with deceptive words; for a long time their judgment has not been idle, and their destruction does not slumber (2 Pet. 2:1-3).

Pastor John MacArthur said:

> The faith healers and health-and-wealth preachers who dominate religious television are shameless frauds. Their message is not the true Gospel of Jesus Christ. There is nothing spiritual or miraculous about their on-stage chicanery. It is all a devious ruse designed to take advantage of desperate people. They are not Godly ministers but greedy impostors who corrupt the Word of God for money's sake. They are not real pastors who shepherd the flock of God but hirelings whose only design is to fleece the sheep. Their love of money is glaringly obvious in what they say as well as how they live. They claim to possess great spiritual power, but in reality they are rank materialists and enemies of everything holy.[2]

Increase in Homosexuality

The Bible prophesies that homosexuality will be increasingly evident at the end of the age: "Without natural affection, trucebreakers, false accusers, incontinent, fierce, despisers of those that are good" (2 Tim. 3:3, *KJV*). We understand this from the phrase "without natural affection," which is the English wording of the Greek word *astorgos*, meaning "without family love." In recent years in our society the family has been redefined. The family is no longer characterized as a mother and a father raising children. *The New York Times* said:

> What is a "family"? Statistically, it is no longer a mother, a father and their biological children living together under one roof (and certainly not with Dad going off to work and Mom staying home). Although perception and acceptance often lag behind reality, there is evidence that a new definition of family—while far from universally accepted—is emerging. A report this month by the Pew Research Center asked 2,691 randomly chosen adults whether seven trends were "good, bad or of no consequence to society." The trends were: more unmarried couples raising children; more gay and lesbian couples raising children.[3]

The same wording "without natural affection" is used in Romans 1:27 in the context of homosexuality: "And likewise also the men, leaving the natural use of the woman, burned in their lust one toward another; men with men working that which is unseemly" (*KJV*).

According to a 2011 study by the Williams Institute at the UCLA School of Law, 9 million (about 3.8 percent) of Americans identify themselves as gay, lesbian, bisexual or transgender. The institute also found that bisexuals make up 1.8 percent of the population, while 1.7 percent are gay or lesbian. Transgender adults make up 0.3 percent of the population.[4]

A Gallup poll stated that "U.S. adults, on average, estimate that 25 percent of Americans are gay or lesbian. More specifically, over half of Americans (52 percent) estimate that at least one in five Americans are gay or lesbian, including 35 percent who estimate that more than one in four are. Thirty percent put the figure at less than 15 percent."[5]

However, the number of Americans who say they have a close friend or family member who is gay jumped from 49 percent in 2010 to 60 percent today. According to an article from CNN, "In the 1990s, most Americans said they did not know anyone close to them who was gay. Attitudes about sexual orientation have also changed over that same time period. In 1998, a majority believed that someone who is homosexual could change their sexual orientation if they chose to do so. Today, only a third feel that way, and the number who say that gays cannot change their orientation is almost six in 10."[6]

Earthquakes Will Be Prevalent

It is written too that earthquakes will be in diverse places: "For nation will rise against nation, and kingdom against kingdom. And there will be famines, pestilences, and earthquakes in various places" (Matt. 24:7).

The Scriptures don't necessarily speak of an *increase* in earthquake activity but of earthquakes happening in different places. The USGS reports:

> We continue to be asked by many people throughout the world if earthquakes are on the increase. Although it may seem that we are having more earthquakes, earthquakes of magnitude 7.0 or greater have remained fairly constant. A partial explanation may lie in the fact that in the last twenty years, we have definitely had an increase in the number of earthquakes we have been able to locate each year. This is because of the tremendous increase in the number of seismograph stations in the world and the many improvements in global communications. . . . The NEIC now locates about 20,000 earthquakes each year or approximately 50 per day. Also, because of the improvements in communications and the increased interest in the environment and natural disasters, the public now learns about more earthquakes. According to long-term records (since about 1900), we expect about 17 major

earthquakes (7.0-7.9) and one great earthquake (8.0 or above) in any given year.[7]

Some scientists, however, disagree about a lack of increase in earthquake activity:

> Large earthquakes greater than 8.0 in magnitude have struck the Earth at a record high rate since 2004 but scientists have analyzed the historical record and found that the increase in seismic activity was likely due to mere chance. Peter Shearer at Scripps Institution of Oceanography and Philip Stark at the University of California, Berkeley examined the global frequency of large magnitude earthquakes from 1900 to 2011. They discovered that while the frequency of magnitude 8.0 and higher earthquakes has been slightly elevated since 2004—at a rate of about 1.2 to 1.4 earthquakes per year—the increased rate was not statistically different from what one might expect to see from random chance. The results of the study were published on January 17, 2012 in *Proceedings of the National Academy of Sciences*.[8]

Stress Will Be Part of Living

"But know this, that in the last days perilous times will come" (2 Tim. 3:1). Life was stressful for most of us before the rise of international terrorism with what we called "the stresses of modern living"—fighting the freeways, dealing with inflation, paying high gas prices, and the like. But with the collapse of national economies and threatened food shortages in recent years, millions have found themselves without homes, without jobs and with uncertain and fearful futures.

Wars and Rumors of Wars

Jesus said that one sign of the end of the age would be that wars will erupt: "Nation will rise against nation, and kingdom against kingdom" (Matt. 24:7). Between 1860 and 1945 there were 34 major wars in the world. However, since the Second World War (which took more than 50 million lives), conflicts between nations have greatly increased:

> Since the end of the Second World War in 1945 there have been over 250 major wars in which over 23 million people have been killed, tens of millions made homeless, and countless millions injured and bereaved. In the history of warfare the twentieth century stands out as the bloodiest and most brutal—three times more people have been killed in wars in the last ninety years than in all the previous five hundred.[9]

General Lawlessness
Another sign the Bible gives of the end times is that people will forsake the moral Law (the Ten Commandments), committing adultery, stealing, lying, blaspheming and killing. "And because lawlessness will abound, the love of many will grow cold" (Matt. 24:12).[10]

Sexual Sin
Adultery and fornication, as Scripture said it would (see Matt. 24:14), have become an accepted way of life: "The Census Bureau recently reported that opposite-sex unmarried couples living together jumped 13 percent this year to 7.5 million."[11] A Pew study found that "about 44 percent of people say they have lived with a partner without being married; for 30- to 49-year-olds that share rose to 57 percent."[12]

Theft and Violent Crime
"For men will be lovers of themselves, lovers of money . . . without self-control, brutal" (2 Tim. 3:2-3).

> California got itself into a years-in-the-making jam when it stuffed too many prisoners into too little space. Prison authorities hijacked common areas, such as gymnasiums,

and retrofitted them with rows upon rows of double- and triple-stacked bunks. As living conditions declined, tempers among inmates rose, and violent outbreaks mushroomed. The courts finally stepped in. They ordered the end of overcrowding. But how could the state achieve that? In part, by dumping inmates back onto the streets.[13]

Six million people are under correctional supervision in the U.S.—more than were in Stalin's gulags. The accelerating rate of incarceration over the past few decades is just as startling as the number of people jailed: in 1980, there were about two hundred and twenty people incarcerated for every hundred thousand Americans; by 2010, the number had more than tripled, to seven hundred and thirty-one. No other country even approaches that. In the past two decades, the money that states spend on prisons has risen at six times the rate of spending on higher education.[14]

Hardened Hearts

Notice that Jesus said that because lawlessness would abound, "the love of many will grow cold" (Matt. 24:12). When I was researching material for my book *Hitler, God and the Bible*, I read a quote from a Nazi soldier that horrified me. He wrote to his wife and told her that when he first began shooting Jewish families, his hand would shake. However, after killing many men, women and children, he was now able to keep his hand steady. As his conscience was hardened against the murder of innocent Jews, its voice was silenced so that he was able to kill without any feelings of alarm.

So it is with those who advocate the murder of children in the womb. When my daughter and her friend began to visit their local abortion clinic to gently plead with women who were going to take the life of their child, they were shocked. After going there regularly, any thought was dashed that most of these women didn't really know what they were doing. While some of the women were apprehensive, many of them knew *exactly* what they were doing. They were there to kill their babies, because they didn't want to be inconvenienced by the children. The more America has hailed the lawless (according to God's Law) killing of the unborn as a legal right of women, the harder people's hearts have become, so that now the slaughter of another human being is perceived simply as freedom of choice.

A Form of Godliness

"Having a form of godliness but denying its power. And from such people turn away!" (2 Tim. 3:5). Scripture speaks of a time in which people will have a belief in God but will deny His power. That effectively describes the hundreds of millions who fill both Catholic and Protestant churches each week, going through a form of religious worship, thinking that suffering on a hard pew for an hour will earn them a place in Heaven. These millions hold God at a distance so that they can enjoy the pleasures of sin, something commonly called hypocrisy.

Back in 1996 a survey conducted by the Alan Guttmacher Institute in New York found that "18 percent of abortion patients describe themselves as born-again or evangelical Christians." A study conducted on evangelical teens found that 66 percent had lied to a parent, 55 percent had had sex, 55 percent had cheated on exams, and 20 percent had gotten drunk or used illegal drugs. Almost 40 percent of pastors who were polled admitted that they'd had an extramarital affair since beginning their ministry. A new study conducted among those in their twenties and thirties who profess to be Christians found that 33 percent believe that cohabitation, gambling, sexual fantasies, abortion, sex outside of marriage, profanity, pornography, same-sex marriage and the use of illegal drugs are morally acceptable.

Santa and Other Myths

Men will substitute fantasy in place of Christian truth: "They will turn their ears away from the truth, and be turned aside to fables" (2 Tim. 4:4). This is evident at Christmas, when the birth of the Savior is lost behind the myth of Santa Claus. According to the Associated Press:

WASHINGTON—Santa has lots going against him—school-yard rumors, older brothers who think they know the deal and tattle to the young ones, errant price tags, the tell-all Internet and so many Made in China labels it seems the North Pole has outsourced to Asia. Humbuggers everywhere. But no worries. It's a wonderful life for Santa. An AP-AOL News poll finds him to be an enduring giant in the lives of Americans. Fully 86 percent in the poll believed in Santa as a child. And despite the multiethnic nature of the country, more than 60 percent of those with children at home consider Santa important in their holiday celebrations now.[15]

Then there is the idea of evolution. I have found that those who embrace the theory of evolution—those who think that they are apes—think like apes. They are *primitive* in their thinking. The theory of evolution is a fable, yet it's preached as gospel truth by millions of its staunch believers. A fable is "a short tale to teach a moral lesson, often with animals or inanimate objects as characters" or "a story not founded on fact."[16] The theory of Darwinian evolution rests on nothing but blind faith. It is believed worldwide, and, like the earth, it hangs on nothing.

Increase of Deadly Diseases

Deadly diseases will be prevalent in the last days: "And there will be . . . pestilences" (Matt. 24:7). The word "pestilence" is defined as "a deadly or virulent epidemic disease."

The influenza commonly called "Spanish flu" killed more people than the guns of World War I. Estimates put the worldwide death toll at 21,642,274. Some one billion people were affected by the disease—half of the total human population. It came at a time when 19 nations were at war and the disruption, stress, and privation of war certainly aided the flu's transmission. It killed people on every continent except Antarctica, with the most lives lost in Asia and the highest percentage of population killed in India.

From August 1918, when cases of the flu started looking abnormally high, until the following July when they returned to about normal, 20 million Americans became sick and more than 500,000 died. In October, 1918, the flu reached its peak, killing about 195,000 Americans. About 57,000 American soldiers died from influenza while the U.S. was at war; about 53,500 died in battle.[17]

The worldwide increase in AIDS deaths is almost inestimable. "Since the beginning of the HIV/AIDS epidemic, 60 million people have contracted HIV."[18]

"Towards an HIV Cure" [is] a global scientific strategy by an international working group of 300 researchers who are developing a road map of sorts, outlining priorities for finding a cure for the disease that has claimed approximately 30 million lives worldwide.[19]

Cancer is a leading cause of death globally: an estimated 7.6 million people died of cancer in 2005 and 84 million people will die in the next 10 years if action is not taken. The World Health Organization (WHO) has proposed a global goal of reducing chronic disease death rates by 2 percent per annum from 2006 to 2015. Achievement of this goal would avert over 8 million of the projected 84 million deaths due to cancer in the next decade.[20]

A seasonal, respiratory infection, flu is responsible for about three to five million cases of severe illness, and about 250,000 to 500,000 deaths, according to the World Health Organization. Periodically, however, the viral infection becomes much more devastating: A pandemic in 1918 killed about 50 million people worldwide.[21]

Denial of a Worldwide Flood

"For this they willfully forget: that by the word of God the heavens were of old, and the earth standing out of water and in the water, by which the world that then existed perished, being flooded with water" (2 Pet. 3:5-6). The fact that God once flooded the earth (in the Noahic flood) will be denied in the end times. There is a mass of fossil evidence to prove this fact, yet it is flatly ignored by the scientific world because of its uncanny implication:

> Evidence of Noah's Flood can be seen all over the earth, from seabeds to mountaintops. Whether you travel by car, train, or plane, the physical features of the earth's terrain clearly indicate a catastrophic past, from canyons and craters to coal beds and caverns. Some layers of strata extend across continents, revealing the effects of a huge catastrophe. The earth's crust has massive amounts of layered sedimentary rock, sometimes miles (kilometers) deep! These layers of sand, soil, and material—mostly laid down by water—were once soft like mud, but they are now hard stone. Encased in these sedimentary layers are billions of dead things (fossils of plants and animals) buried very quickly. The evidence all over the earth is staring everyone in the face.[22]

The Institution of Marriage Will Be Rejected

The institution of marriage will also be abandoned by many: "In latter times some will depart from the faith, . . . forbidding to marry" (1 Tim. 4:1,3). In the United Kingdom, according to the BBC:

> Fewer people believe couples should get married before starting a family. The annual survey by the National Centre for Social Research published this week found that in 1989 seven out of 10 people believed children should be born in wedlock, but now only 54 percent do. A clear majority (67 percent) thought cohabitation was acceptable, even if a couple did not intend to get married.[23]

In the United States marriage is no longer relevant to millions:

> About 29 percent of children under 18 now live with a parent or parents who are unwed or no longer married, a fivefold

increase from 1960, according to the Pew report being released Thursday. Broken down further, about 15 percent have parents who are divorced or separated and 14 percent who were never married. Within those two groups, a sizable chunk—6 percent—have parents who are live-in couples who opted to raise kids together without getting married. Indeed, about 39 percent of Americans said marriage was becoming obsolete. And that sentiment follows U.S. census data released in September that showed marriages hit an all-time low of 52 percent for adults 18 and over. In 1978, just 28 percent believed marriage was becoming obsolete.[24]

Famine Increase

There will be an increase in famines: "And there will be famines" (Matt. 24:7).

November 11, 2002: "Ethiopia is facing a famine that could affect as many as 15 million people, the country's prime minister has warned. Meles Zenawi called for urgent international aid to help avoid a catastrophe on a scale that would dwarf the country's 1984-85 famine."[25]

August 30, 2009: "Millions facing famine in Ethiopia as rains fail. International aid agencies fear that the levels of death and starvation last seen 24 years ago, are set to return to the Horn of Africa."[26]

May 30, 2010: "10 million face famine in West Africa. Drought and failing harvests bring new fears of a food disaster in two sub-Saharan countries."[27]

September 5, 2011: "The United Nations announced Monday that Somalia's famine had spread to a sixth area within the country, with officials warning that 750,000 people could die in the next few months unless aid efforts were scaled up."[28]

The Popularity of Vegetarianism

The Scriptures tell us that vegetarianism will increase. There will be those who command people "to abstain from foods which God created to be received with thanksgiving by those who believe and know the truth. For every creature of God is good, and nothing is to be refused if it is received with thanksgiving" (1 Tim. 4:3-4).

The just-released "Vegetarianism in America" study, published by *Vegetarian Times* (vegetariantimes.com), shows that 3.2 percent of U.S. adults, or 7.3 million people, follow a vegetarian-based diet. Approximately 0.5 percent, or 1 million, of those are vegans, who consume no animal products at all. In addition, 10 percent of U.S. adults, or 22.8 million people, say they largely follow a vegetarian-inclined diet.[29]

The Jerusalem Headache

The possession of Jerusalem will also be at the center of international turmoil: "And in that day will I make Jerusalem a burdensome stone for all people: all that burden themselves with it shall be cut in pieces, though all the people of the earth be gathered together against it" (Zech. 12:3, *KJV*).

Headlines and reports such as the following have become commonplace:

Jerusalem Is at the Center of Another Conflict: Separation of Powers.[30]

Police presence high in volatile east Jerusalem: Palestinians and police clashed repeatedly this past week in east Jerusalem. The violence coincided with a U.S.-Israeli diplomatic feud.[31]

WASHINGTON—Members of the International Israel Allies Caucus Foundation met in Washington, D.C., this week and called on the United States to recognize Jerusalem as the undivided capital of Israel. Jerusalem's ties to the Jewish people date back at least 3,000 years, to King David's reign.

The city is mentioned 600 times in the Bible's Old Testament and another 160 times in the New Testament. It is never mentioned in the Koran.[32]

JERUSALEM—Israeli officials are dismissing announcements by the International Atomic Energy Agency (IAEA) of yet another "breakthrough" in diplomatic efforts to halt Iran's suspected nuclear weapons program. . . . Israeli Defense Minister Ehud Barak seemed flabbergasted that the IAEA would once again fall for what he and other Israeli leaders see as obvious delaying tactics by Iran. "The Iranians are trying to reach a technical deal that will create the appearance of progress in the talks in order to alleviate [international] pressure . . . and postpone an escalation in sanctions," Barak said, as he urged the West to stop playing the willful idiot in this scenario.[33]

The city of Jerusalem is a powder keg, surrounded by the fires of militant Islam. It is a continual and painful headache for the United Nations, which doesn't want to clash with oil-rich Islamic nations whose passionate public agenda is to annihilate Israel. Militant Muslims want Jerusalem to be Islam's holy capital:

In a speech published on his website Thursday, Iranian President Mahmoud Ahmadinejad said the ultimate goal of world forces must be the annihilation of Israel. Speaking to ambassadors from Islamic countries ahead of "Qods Day" ("Jerusalem Day"), an annual Iranian anti-Zionist event established in 1979 by Ayatollah Khomeini and which falls this year on August 17, Ahmadinejad said that a "horrible Zionist current" had been managing world affairs for "about 400 years."[34]

Increase in Knowledge

In the last days, Scripture tells us that knowledge will increase: "But you, Daniel, shut up the words, and seal the book until the time of the end; many shall run to and fro, and knowledge shall increase" (Dan. 12:4).

Darren Hardy, the publisher of *Success* magazine, said:

There are only a few certainties in life: death, taxes . . . and change. And the rate of change is speeding up—rapidly. Several factors are causing this acceleration: the expansion of technology and knowledge, globalization and the changing demographic majority. Let's take a look at how these factors are impacting the landscape of leadership. Technology: Ray Kurzweil, in his 2001 essay "The Law of Accelerating Returns," asserts that technology won't experience 100 years of progress in the 21st century—it will be more like 20,000 years of progress (at today's rate). Knowledge: By 1900, it had taken 150 years to double all human knowledge. Today it takes only one or two years, and by 2020, knowledge will double every 72 days, according to estimates.[35]

Other signs of the end of the age will include an increase of religious cults and false teachers: "Then many false prophets will rise up and deceive many" (Matt. 24:11; see also 24:24). The future will seem fearful to many, "men's hearts failing them from fear and the expectation of those things which are coming on the earth" (Luke 21:26). Humanity will become materialistic (see 2 Tim. 3:4). There will be many involved in travel (see Dan. 12:4)—think of the massive revolution in travel with the advent of the train, car and plane. The Christian gospel will be preached as a warning to all nations (see Matt. 24:14), and Jesus cautioned that Christians will be hated for His name's sake (see Matt. 24:9). Youth will become rebellious: "For men will be lovers of themselves, lovers of money, boasters, proud, blasphemers, disobedient to parents, unthankful, unholy" (2 Tim. 3:2).

If you are thinking that these signs have always been around and that they are nothing new, you may have become part of the fulfillment of Bible prophecy: "Scoffers will come in the last days . . . saying, 'Where is the promise of His coming? For since the fathers fell asleep, all things continue as they were from the beginning of the creation'" (2 Pet. 3:3-4). Matthew Henry said of this passage:

> The purified minds of Christians are to be stirred up, that they may be active and lively in the work of holiness. There will be scoffers in the last days, under the gospel, men who make light of sin, and mock at salvation by Jesus Christ. One very principal article of our faith refers to what only has a promise to rest upon, and scoffers will attack it till our Lord is come. They will not believe that he will come. Because they see no changes, therefore they fear not God, Ps 55:19. What he never has done, they fancy he never can do, or never will do.[36]

The Bible even reveals the motivation of those who mock—a love for the sin of lust (see 2 Pet. 3:3). Those who mock fail to understand that a day to the Lord is as a thousand years to us. As we have seen, God isn't subject to the time that He has created. He can look forward into time as we look back through the pages of a history book. The reason He seems to be silent is that He is patiently waiting, not willing that any perish but that all come to repentance (see 2 Pet. 3:9).

THE TIMELINE

Here now is the "timeline" for all these signs and for the end of the age—for the second coming of Jesus Christ. Jesus said that we would know that we are at the door of His coming when the Jews obtain Jerusalem:

> But woe to those who are pregnant and to those who are nursing babies in those days! For there will be great distress in the land and wrath upon this people. And they will fall by the edge of the sword, and be led away captive into all nations. And Jerusalem will be trampled by Gentiles until the times of the Gentiles are fulfilled (Luke 21:23-25).

In other words, Jesus was saying that Jerusalem was going to fall to the Gentiles and would be overrun by them for a period of time. But when the times of the Gentiles were fulfilled, the Jews would regain the city of Jerusalem, which would herald the coming of the end of the age and the soon return of Jesus Christ to the earth.

So that we can understand the context of this passage, let's look back a few verses. In Luke 21:6 we see that Jesus had told the disciples that the Jerusalem temple would be destroyed, and the disciples had then asked Jesus, "Teacher, but when will these things be? And what sign will there be when these things are about to take place?" (21:7). Jesus told them that there would be deceivers who would come in His name, wars, nation rising against nation, earthquakes in various places, famines, pestilences, fearful sights and great signs from Heaven (see 21:8-11).

Then in verse 12, we see that Jesus had said, "But before all these things..." Jesus was emphasizing that something else would take place *before* all these terrible things happened. What would happen before the wars, earthquakes and famines? Three things: (1) Christian persecution (see 21:12-19), (2) the terrible destruction of Jerusalem (see 21:20), (3) and the dispersion of the Jews throughout all nations (see 21:21). So first there would be terrible persecution, the destruction of Jerusalem and the dispersion of the Jews; then would come the signs of earthquakes, wars and famines. Following that would come the destruction of Jerusalem by the Gentiles, which took place in AD 70, just 40 years after Jesus made these statements.

The historian Josephus claimed that during the AD 70 siege of Jerusalem by Rome, 1,100,000 people were killed, of which a majority were Jewish, and 97,000 were captured and enslaved. He wrote:

> Now as soon as the army had no more people to slay or to plunder, because there remained none to be the objects of their fury (for they would not have spared any, had there remained any other work to be done), [Titus] Caesar gave orders that they should now demolish the entire city and Temple, but should leave as many of the towers standing

as they were of the greatest eminence . . . but for all the
rest of the wall [surrounding Jerusalem], it was so thoroughly laid even with the ground by those that dug it up
to the foundation, that there was left nothing to make
those that came thither believe it [Jerusalem] had ever
been inhabited. This was the end which Jerusalem came
to by the madness of those that were for innovations; a
city otherwise of great magnificence, and of mighty fame
among all mankind.[37]

Jesus had warned about this event 40 years before it happened:
"But woe to those who are pregnant and to those who are nursing
babies in those days! For there will be great distress in the land
and wrath upon this people" (Luke 21:23).

The slaughter within was even more dreadful than the
spectacle from without. Men and women, old and young,
insurgents and priests, those who fought and those who
entreated mercy, were hewn down in indiscriminate car-
nage. The number of the slain exceeded that of the slay-
ers. The legionaries had to clamber over heaps of dead to
carry on the work of extermination.[38]

Jerusalem was indeed destroyed, just as Jesus had said, and the
Jews were scattered thorough the nations, left without a homeland.
    In the late 1800s and early 1900s—almost 2,000 years after
their dispersion—the Jews began moving back to the land of Israel.
Ironically, the destruction of Jerusalem in AD 70 had begun with a
siege, and as Israel fought to reestablish a hold on the city in 1948,
Arab forces also laid siege to it:

Starting in early 1948, the Arab forces had severed the supply line to Jewish Jerusalem. On March 31, the head of the
Jerusalem Emergency Committee, Dov Yosef, introduced
a draconian system of food rationing. The bread ration
was 200 grams per person. The April Passover week ration

per person was 2 pounds of potatoes, 2 eggs, 0.5 pounds fish, 4 pounds matzoth, 1.5 ounces dried fruit, 0.5 pounds meat and 0.5 pounds matza flour. The meat cost one Palestinian pound per pound. On May 12, water rationing was introduced. . . . When convoys bearing foodstuffs could not reach the city, the residents of Jerusalem went out to the fields to pick mallow leaves, which are rich in iron and vitamins. The Jerusalem radio station, Kol Hamagen, broadcast instructions for cooking mallow. When the broadcasts were picked up in Jordan, they sparked victory celebrations. Radio Amman announced that the fact that the Jews were eating leaves, which was food for donkeys and cattle, was a sign that they were dying of starvation and would soon surrender.[39]

But after approximately 19 centuries during which the Gentiles maintained control of Jerusalem, the Jews finally obtained Israel in 1948 and then the city of Jerusalem in 1967. This was the sign of which Jesus had spoken that would show us God's calendar regarding the end of the age.

For nearly 2,000 years Jerusalem had been "trodden down of the Gentiles" (Luke 21:24, *KJV*). It was in non-Jewish hands until 1967, when the Jews miraculously obtained possession of the city. This brought about the culmination of all the signs of the times of which the Bible speaks. We are now at the end of the age, close to the coming of Jesus Christ.

THE GREAT HOPE

The second coming of Jesus is the hope of every Christian. We long for God to put a stop to suffering and death. We ache for Him to stop the murders, the wars and rapes, the slaughter of children in the womb, and the agendas of evil men and women. We want the promised new heavens and new earth in which there will be no earthquakes, famines, tornados, hurricanes, disease or death. When these are established, God's kingdom will come to this earth and God's will shall be done on this earth as it is in Heaven.

We have all heard the saying, "If it sounds too good to be true, it probably is." That's wise advice when we are dealing with sinful man. But we can forget that saying when it comes to the promises of God. He is faithful. He will bless those who trust in His mercy and will punish those who die in their sins. If your sins are forgiven, you will love His appearing (see 2 Tim. 4:8).

But if you have refused to obey the command to repent and are not trusting Jesus Christ, look at this fearful warning:

> We are bound to thank God always for you, brethren, as it is fitting, because your faith grows exceedingly, and the love of every one of you all abounds toward each other, so that we ourselves boast of you among the churches of God for your patience and faith in all your persecutions and tribulations that you endure, which is manifest evidence of the righteous judgment of God, that you may be counted worthy of the kingdom of God, for which you also suffer; since it is a righteous thing with God to repay with tribulation those who trouble you, and to give you who are troubled rest with us when the Lord Jesus is revealed from heaven with His mighty angels, in flaming fire taking vengeance on those who do not know God, and on those who do not obey the gospel of our Lord Jesus Christ. These shall be punished with everlasting destruction from the presence of the Lord and from the glory of His power, when He comes, in that Day, to be glorified in His saints and to be admired among all those who believe, because our testimony among you was believed (2 Thess. 1:3-10).

It's a fearful thing to fall into the hands of the living God.

JOB AND LOVE

Job 42:7-17

I am painfully aware that this book falls short of providing a complete answer to the question of human suffering. God left Job in the dark when it came to this question, but He didn't leave him without light in his darkness. And we too have enough light in our suffering, because we have access to the light of life (see John 8:12). For the time being, that light is sufficient for us.

An Internet search will yield heartbreaking pictures of children whose limbs have been torn from their burned bodies because of war. We will find photos of grieving mothers at their children's bedsides as they try to comfort them in their agony. Where is God in such anguish? Where is He when babies are born with terrible deformities or when people suffer in quiet despair from severe mental illness? Where is God when people are murdered or tortured to death or when millions are slaughtered in events such as the Holocaust or though abortion? Did these millions of ill-fated human beings suffer because God had told Satan that they were upright before Him?

The answer is that we don't know why these things happen. And even though we as Christians are able to lift ourselves above the knowledge of these horrors by trusting God, that is of little consolation to those unbelievers who are suffering. But those who look to God and seek out the truth of His Word can trust the Lord, because these awful incidents confirm to us that we live in a fallen creation, and we realize that most of these hurtful things happen

because of the evil nature of human beings. We can be assured of
the fact that despite these terrible realities of life, God is without
blame. This is what Job discovered in his trial, and this is the comfort we can take away from the Scriptures:

> For whatever things were written before were written for
> our learning, that we through the patience and comfort
> of the Scriptures might have hope (Rom. 15:4).

Samuel Chadwick said, "No man is uneducated who knows
the Bible, and no one is wise who is ignorant of its teachings." If
you are in some fiery trial, soak your soul in the soothing balm of
the Bible's psalms. Draw close to God through prayer, and despite
the pain in your life, let the heat you are going through purify you
as gold. Offer God the "*sacrifice* of praise" (Heb. 13:15, emphasis
added). Worship Him in the lion's den. The book of Hebrews tells
us about certain individuals who had the kind of faith that
"stopped the mouth of lions":

> By faith the walls of Jericho fell down after they were encir-
> cled for seven days. By faith the harlot Rahab did not per-
> ish with those who did not believe, when she had received
> the spies with peace.
>   And what more shall I say? For the time would fail me
> to tell of Gideon and Barak and Samson and Jephthah,
> also of David and Samuel and the prophets: who through
> faith subdued kingdoms, worked righteousness, obtained
> promises, stopped the mouths of lions, quenched the vio-
> lence of fire, escaped the edge of the sword, out of weak-
> ness were made strong, became valiant in battle, turned to
> flight the armies of the aliens. Women received their dead
> raised to life again.
>   Others were tortured, not accepting deliverance, that
> they might obtain a better resurrection. Still others had
> trial of mockings and scourgings, yes, and of chains and
> imprisonment. They were stoned, they were sawn in two,

were tempted, were slain with the sword. They wandered about in sheepskins and goatskins, being destitute, afflicted, tormented—of whom the world was not worthy. They wandered in deserts and mountains, in dens and caves of the earth.

And all these, having obtained a good testimony through faith, did not receive the promise, God having provided something better for us, that they should not be made perfect apart from us (Heb. 11:30-40).

In our fearful times, we can either look at the lion's teeth or look to God. Our peace will be in proportion to our faith. We can let God be glorified in our suffering by trust in His promises.

WHAT WOULD YOU MISS?

Let me ask you some soul-searching questions. Besides your loved ones, what do you value most in life? Is it your eyesight? If you knew that you were going to die at midnight tonight, would you mourn the fact that you would never again see the sunrise? Or perhaps you most value your ability to feel things. If you lost this, would you be sad that you would no longer be able to feel the warmth of the sun's rays? Or perhaps instead you would miss the enjoyment of a satisfyingly cool drink on a hot day or the taste of a tender steak or the sound of good music.

When we give it a little thought, life has many pleasures that we would dearly miss if they were suddenly taken from us. Every one of these pleasures that we enjoy—color, music, food, drink, love and laughter—comes from God. But the same God who blesses us with beautiful things also curses and punishes. Keep in mind that while it was Satan who killed Job's servants and children and who covered Job with boils, God was the One who had ultimate control over Job's situation. He is completely sovereign. And for that we need never apologize. The Scriptures don't:

Then all his brothers, all his sisters, and all those who had been his acquaintances before, came to him and ate food with him in his house; and they consoled him and comforted him for all the adversity that the LORD had brought upon him (Job 42:11).

It was the Lord who had brought all the adversity on Job, and all God's judgments are righteous and true altogether.

Keeping in mind the thought of God's power over our circumstances, consider the pains we all experience in life. Think of unbearable pounding headaches, screaming earaches, excruciating back pain, agonizing bee stings, severe knee pain, kidney stones, throbbing toothaches, the torment of a nightmare from which we wake up panting with horror, having a pounding heart and a sweating brow. Think of the terrible ache caused by a broken bone, a pulled muscle or a throbbing infection in a swollen wound. All these dreadful things are merely the body's reaction to negative experiences in a fallen creation—and our bodies, which can feel all these pains, were created by a loving and kind God. God created the spinal cord that registers pain. He made the mind that experiences nightmares. He gave the tooth those nerves that enable us to feel the dentist's drill.

While God does allow us to experience distress, the pains we feel aren't *punishment* from God for sin. They come as a result of everyday life in a fallen creation. If we fall, we get hurt. If we eat too much cheese at night, get too hot in bed, watch a scary movie or harbor hidden fears, we have nightmares. The assessment of Job's three friends that God was punishing Job for his sins was erroneous. In fact, the Lord corrected them for their mistaken appraisal: "The LORD said to Eliphaz the Temanite, 'My wrath is aroused against you and your two friends, for you have not spoken of Me what is right, as My servant Job has'" (Job 42:7). Job's suffering, even though it had been arranged by the devil in an attempt to make Job curse God, was not God's punishment against him but simply a result of living in this broken, sinful world.

But listen to me with the soberest of hearts—Hell will be a place in which God *punishes* human beings for crimes committed against His Law. The terrible endurance of Hell will be much worse than the mere pains of this life, because (I say this reverently) God knows exactly how to hit a raw nerve. Hell will unleash the fury of almighty God against the multitude of our sins, and the Bible understates it when it warns, "It's a fearful thing to fall into the hands of the living God" (Heb. 10:31).

One of the most common retorts of the unthinking ungodly is that they do not mind the thought of going to Hell. But Hell will not simply be a place in which we lose all our valued blessings and remember with longing the things we miss most; it will be a place in which God gives sinners exactly what they deserve. When Job despaired of life, he had the consolation that death would take him out of his nightmare. But Hell goes beyond death—it is an everlasting nightmare. *It will never end.* It will be worse than an unbearable toothache from which there will be no relief or an agonizing broken bone for which there is no healing.

If Hell didn't exist, I would not be writing these sobering words. Even if Hell had an end, I could say, "World, go to Hell—I really don't care." But I know that Hell is going to be much, much worse than this pain-filled life. So I write books and do everything I can to warn this world about it, because I'm horrified that my worst enemy could end up there. Please don't die in your sins. I plead with you, cry out to God in repentance, and flee to the Savior to have your sins forgiven.

THE PAIN OF EMPATHY

For those of us who have been saved and set free from our sin, God calls us to take the gospel to those who have not yet received Him. This might cost us. It might hurt. But since the love of God has so transformed our own lives and futures, how can we not reach out to others who are in danger of the fires of Hell with that same love? How can we not empathize with them in their plight?

Empathy is more than sympathy or even compassion. It enters into the pain of people who are victims of suffering. Psychologists tell us that a psychotic killer lacks the virtue of empathy, which is reflected in the fact that such a killer usually considers himself to be number one in the universe. *Do you have empathy? Are you pained by the fate of the unsaved? Do you love sinners?* The Scriptures say, "He who does not love does not know God, for God is love" (1 John 4:8).

I have a confession to make. When I was a new Christian, I was like a man possessed. I had been graciously rescued from a sure death itself by the "Jaws of Life" in Christ. I had been given the gift of everlasting life! Death had lost its terrible sting. I exploded with gratitude to God, but I also had an all-consuming empathy for those who were still sitting in the shadow of death and were to be cast into Hell. I could not, I dared not, keep quiet about the gospel of God's mercy in Christ. I purchased a printing press and printed tracts. I procured a huge bus and had a professional sign-writer put Scriptures all over it. I did the same with my car. I put a Bible billboard in our front yard. I put huge Bible verses on the window of my store, gave out tracts wherever I went and daily preached in the open air to the unsaved.

As a new a Christian, I could certainly have been considered a fanatic. That was more than 40 years ago, and you know what? *Today I'm worse!* Much worse. I use international television and radio to reach the lost. I rent huge billboards, hire sky-signs and print tracts by the millions, and I give out the tracts wherever I go. I daily blog, tweet, Facebook, write books, give away DVDs, witness to whoever will listen, and preach in the open air.

But I consider myself to be less than a *normal* biblical Christian. When I look at the book of Acts, the disciples make me look lukewarm. They were hated, stoned and tortured, and many of them valiantly gave their precious lives in martyrdom to take the gospel to a lost and dying world.

Many of the disciples voluntarily put themselves into a Job experience. Not only did they *accept* suffering as a part of this life, but also they *embraced* it. They willingly gave up their finances, their families, their food, their friends and their freedom to follow Jesus Christ. Paul was beaten, stoned, shipwrecked and left alone in prison until the executioner came to take his life. But he said:

Yet indeed I also count all things loss for the excellence of the knowledge of Christ Jesus my Lord, for whom I have suffered the loss of all things, and count them as rubbish, that I may gain Christ (Phil. 3:8).

Paul was treated cruelly, thrown in prison, horribly stoned and left for dead. But we don't see him asking God why He had allowed such suffering. Paul never once pointed an accusing finger at his perfect Creator. He rather put his priorities in order:

Even though our outward man is perishing, yet the inward man is being renewed day by day. For our light affliction, which is but for a moment, is working for us a far more exceeding and eternal weight of glory, while we do not look at the things which are seen, but at the things which are not seen. For the things which are seen are temporary, but the things which are not seen are eternal (2 Cor. 4:16-18).

To Paul, any suffering was merely a "light affliction," and it was only for "a moment." The Scriptures don't make light *of* our pain; they give us light *in* it. The Bible contrasts the experiences we have in this life with the unending pleasure we will have in eternity. Job's story gives us a picture of this. Although Job endured terrible, unexplainable agony for a season, in the end "the LORD blessed the latter days of Job more than his beginning; for he had fourteen thousand sheep, six thousand camels, one thousand yoke of oxen, and one thousand female donkeys. He also had seven sons and three daughters" (Job 42:12-13). Do you believe that our eternal reward will outweigh any pain we experience now? As a Christian, do you believe that God is working in every trial for your good?

Remember, if you are trusting in the Savior, any suffering you go through isn't punishment for your sins; it is an occurrence for your good. You haven't angered God. But He has allowed your trials for a reason, so don't look at the things that are seen but at the things that are eternal. I have committed the following faith-building and encouraging portion of Scripture to memory. I suggest you do the same:

Blessed be the God and Father of our Lord Jesus Christ, which according to his abundant mercy hath begotten us again unto a lively hope by the resurrection of Jesus Christ from the dead, to an inheritance incorruptible, and unde-filed, and that fadeth not away, reserved in heaven for you, who are kept by the power of God through faith unto sal-vation ready to be revealed in the last time. Wherein ye greatly rejoice, though now for a season, if need be, ye are in heaviness through manifold temptations: that the trial of your faith, being much more precious than of gold that perishes, though it be tried with fire, might be found unto praise and honour and glory at the appearing of Jesus Christ; whom having not seen, ye love; in whom, though now ye see him not, yet believing, ye rejoice with joy un-speakable and full of glory. Receiving the end of your faith, even the salvation of your souls (1 Pet. 1:3-9, *KJV*).

Job said that he had heard of God by the hearing of his ear, but after His Creator spoke, he said, "But now my eye sees You!" (Job 42:5). Has God spoken to you? Have you caught a glimpse of His holiness, and has that produced in you a healthy fear of God? Then may I ask, despite any pain you may be going through, that you look to the lost? If you can't preach to crowds of unsaved peo-ple, witness to people one on one. If you can't do that, then give out gospel tracts. Whatever you do, do something to reach the mil-lions who are destined for a terrifying place that will make every af-fliction on this earth seem like a Sunday School picnic. As Christians, we have been called to the most serious business—our *Father's* business. We have been commissioned to preach the gospel of salvation—the message of everlasting life—given to us from the mouth of God.

SAVE YOURSELF SOME PAIN

It is my sincere hope that you have made peace with God through trusting in Jesus Christ. Becoming a Christian is the most incredible event that will ever take place in your life. If you have obeyed the gospel by turning from your sins and placing your trust in Jesus Christ alone for your salvation, you have found everlasting life (see John 3:16; Rom. 6:23; 10:9-13; 1 John 5:11-12). Be assured, God will never leave you nor forsake you. He has brought you this far, and He will complete the wonderful work He has begun in you. He knows your every thought, your every care and your deepest concerns.

Let's look at some of those concerns that you may have. First, and of primary concern, do you have "assurance" of your salvation? The Bible says to "make every effort to confirm your calling and election" (2 Pet. 1:10, *KJV*), so let's go through a short checklist to make sure that you are truly saved:

- Are you aware that God became flesh in the person of Jesus Christ (see 1 Tim. 3:16) and that He died for the sins of the world?
- Did you come to the Savior because you knew that you had sinned against God?
- Are you convinced that Jesus suffered and died on the cross for your sins and that He rose again on the third day?
- Did you truly repent (turn from your sin) and put your faith (trust) in Jesus?

God acquits us from the courtroom of eternal justice on the grounds that Jesus Christ has paid our fine. We are justified (made right with God) by Jesus' suffering death. The resurrection of Jesus Christ was God's seal of approval of His sacrifice, signifying that Christ's precious blood was sufficient to pay our fine. If we turn from sin and place our trust in Jesus—the only grounds for forgiveness—God will grant us mercy. However, if you're not sure of your salvation, read Psalm 51 and make it your own prayer.

Following are several important principles that can save you a great deal of pain as you follow Jesus Christ in this fallen world.

1. FEEDING ON THE WORD— DAILY NUTRITION

A healthy baby has a healthy appetite. If you have truly been born of the Spirit of God, you will have a healthy appetite. The Bible says, "As newborn babes, desire the pure milk of the word, that you may grow thereby [in your salvation]" (1 Pet. 2:2). So feed yourself daily by reading the Word of God. The more you eat, the quicker you will grow, and the less bruising you will have. Speed up the process and save yourself some pain—vow to read God's Word every day, without fail. Job said, "I have treasured the words of His mouth more than my necessary food" (Job 23:12). Be like Job, and put your Bible before your belly. Say to yourself, "No Bible, no breakfast. No read, no feed." If you do that, God promises that you will be like a fruitful, strong and healthy tree (see Ps. 1).

Each day find somewhere quiet and thoroughly soak your soul in the Word of God. There may be times when you read through its pages with great enthusiasm and other times when it seems dry and even boring. But food profits your body whether you enjoy it or not. As a child, you no doubt ate desserts with great enthusiasm. Perhaps vegetables weren't so exciting. If you were a normal child, you probably had to be encouraged to eat them at first. Then, as you matured in life, you learned to discipline yourself to eat vegetables. This is because they nourish and strengthen you, even though they may not bring pleasure to your taste buds.

2. FAITH—BECAUSE ELEVATORS CAN LET US DOWN

A young man once said to me, "Ray, I find it hard to believe some of the things in the Bible." I smiled at him and asked, "What's your name?" When he said, "Paul," I casually answered, "I don't believe you." He looked at me questioningly. I repeated, "What's your name?" Again he said, "Paul," and again I answered, "I don't believe you." Then I asked him, "Where do you live?" When he told me, I said, "I don't believe that either." His reaction, understandably, was one of anger. I said, "You look a little upset. Do you know why? You're upset because I didn't believe what you told me. If you tell me that your name is Paul and I say, 'I don't believe you,' it means that I think you are a liar. It means that I think you are trying to deceive me by telling me your name is Paul when it's not."

Then I told him that if he, a mere man, felt insulted by my lack of faith in his word, how much more did he insult almighty God by refusing to believe His Word. In doing so, he was saying that God isn't worth trusting—that He is a liar and a deceiver. The Bible says, "The one who does not believe God has made Him a liar" (1 John 5:10). It also says, "Beware, brethren, lest there be in any of you an evil heart of unbelief in departing from the living God" (Heb. 3:12). Martin Luther said, "What greater insult . . . can there be to God, than not to believe His promises."

I have heard people say, "But I find it hard to have faith in God," not realizing the implications of their words. These are the same people who often accept the daily weather forecast, believe the newspapers and trust their lives to a pilot they have never seen whenever they board a plane. We exercise faith every day. We rely on our car's brakes. We trust history books, medical books and elevators. Yet planes can crash. History books can be wrong. Elevators can let us down. How much more then should we trust the sure and true promises of almighty God. He will never let us down—if we trust Him.

Cynics often argue, "You can't trust the Bible—it's full of mistakes." It is. The first mistake was when man rejected God, and the Scriptures show men and women making the same tragic mistake again and again. The Bible is also full of what seem to be contradictions. For example, the Scriptures tell us that "with God nothing will be impossible" (Luke 1:37), that there is nothing almighty God cannot do. Yet we are also told that "it is impossible for God to lie" (Heb. 6:18). So there is something God cannot do! Isn't that an obvious "mistake" in the Bible? The answer to this dilemma is found in the lowly worm.

Do you know that it would be impossible for me to eat worms? I once saw a man on TV butter a piece of toast and then pour on it a can of live, fat, wriggling, blood-filled worms. He carefully took a knife and fork, cut into his moving meal and ate it. It made me feel sick. It was disgusting. The thought of chewing cold, live worms is to me so repulsive, so distasteful, that I can candidly say that it would be impossible for me to eat them, even though I have seen someone do it. It is so abhorrent that I draw on the strength of the word "impossible" to substantiate my claim.

Lying, deception and bearing false witness are so repulsive to God, so disgusting to Him, so against His holy character, that the Scriptures draw on the strength of the word "impossible" to substantiate the claim that God cannot do them. He cannot, could not and would not lie.

That means that in a world in which we are continually let down, we can totally rely on, trust in and count on His promises. God's promises are sure, certain, indisputable, true, trustworthy, reliable, faithful, unfailing, dependable, steadfast and an anchor for our souls. In other words, we can truly believe them, and because of that, we can throw ourselves blindfolded and without reserve into His mighty hands. He will never, ever let us down. Do you believe that?

3. EVANGELISM—OUR MOST SOBERING TASK

Late in December 1996 a large family gathered in Los Angeles for a joyous Christmas. There were so many gathered that night that five of the children slept in the converted garage, kept warm during the night by an electric heater placed near the door.

During the early hours of the morning, the heater suddenly burst into flames, blocking the doorway. In seconds the room became a blazing inferno. A frantic 911 call revealed unspeakable terror as one of the children could be heard screaming, "I'm on fire!" The distraught father vainly rushed into the flames to try to save his beloved children, receiving burns on 50 percent of his body. Tragically, all five children burned to death. They died because steel bars on the windows had thwarted their escape. There was only one door, and the flames had blocked it.[1]

Imagine you are back in time, standing at the scene of this converted garage just before the heater burst into flames. You peer through the darkness at the peaceful sight of five sleeping youngsters, knowing that at any moment the room will erupt into an inferno and burn the flesh of these horrified children. Can you in good conscience walk away? No! You must awaken the children and warn them to run from that death trap!

The world sleeps peacefully in the darkness of ignorance. There is only one door by which they may escape death. The steel bars of sin prevent their salvation and at the same time call for the flames of eternal justice. What a fearful thing Judgment Day will be! The fires of the wrath of almighty God will burn for eternity. The Church has been entrusted with the task of awakening the lost before it's too late. We cannot turn our backs and walk away in complacency. Think of how the father ran into the flames. His love knew no bounds. Our devotion to the sober task God has given us will be in direct proportion to our love for the lost. There are only a few laborers who run headlong into the flames to warn people to flee (see Luke 10:2). Please be one of them. We really have no choice. The apostle Paul said, "Woe is me if I do not preach the gospel!" (1 Cor. 9:16).

If you and I ignore a drowning child and let him die when we have the ability to save him, we are guilty of the crime of "depraved indifference." God forbid that any Christian should be guilty of that crime when it comes to those around us who are perishing. We have an obligation to reach out to them. The prince of preachers, Charles Spurgeon, said, "Have you no wish for others to be saved? Then you are not saved yourself. Be sure of that."

A Christian cannot be apathetic about the salvation of the world. The love of God in him will motivate him to seek and save that which is lost.

Each of us probably has a limited amount of time after our conversion to impact our unsaved friends and family with the gospel. After the initial shock of our conversion, those who know us will put us in a neat little ribbon-tied box and keep us at arm's length. So it's important that we take advantage of the short time we have while we still have their ears.

Here's some advice that may save you a great deal of grief. As a new Christian, I did almost irreparable damage by acting like a wild bull in a crystal showroom. I bullied my mom, my dad and many of my friends into making a decision for Christ. I was sincere, zealous, loving, kind and stupid. I didn't understand that salvation doesn't come through making a decision but through repentance, nor did I understand that repentance is God-given (see 2 Tim. 2:25). The Bible teaches that no one can come to the Son unless the Father draws him (see John 6:44). If you are able to get a decision from someone but the person has no conviction of sin, you will almost certainly end up with a stillborn on your hands.

In my "enthusiasm without knowledge" (Prov. 19:2, *NLT*), I actually inoculated the very ones I was so desperately trying to reach. As new Christians, there is nothing more important to us than the salvation of our loved ones, and we don't want to blow it. If we do, we may find that we don't have a second chance. Fervently pray for your family members and friends, asking God for their salvation. Let them see your faith. Let them feel your kindness, your genuine love and your gentleness. Buy them gifts for no reason. Do chores for them when you are not asked to. Go the extra mile. Put yourself in their position. You know that you have found everlasting life—death has lost its sting! Your joy is unspeakable. But as far as they are concerned, you've been brainwashed and have become part of a weird sect. Your loving actions will speak more loudly to them than 10,000 eloquent sermons.

For this reason you should avoid verbal confrontation until you have the knowledge to guide your zeal. Pray for wisdom and for sensitivity to God's timing. You may have only one shot, so make it count. Keep your cool. If you don't, you may end up with a lifetime of regret. Believe me. It is better to hear a loved one or a close friend say, "Tell me about your faith in Jesus Christ," than for you to say, "Sit down. I want to talk to you." Continue to persevere in prayer for your loves ones that God would open their eyes to the truth.

Remember also that you have the sobering responsibility of speaking to other people's loved ones. Perhaps another Christian has prayed earnestly that God would use a faithful witness to speak to his beloved mom or dad, and you are the answer to that believer's prayer. You are the true and faithful witness God wants to use. We should share our faith with others whenever we can. The Bible says that we should proclaim the message and "persist in it whether convenient or not" (2 Tim. 4:2, *HCSB*).

Never lose sight of the world and all its pains. Keep the fate of the ungodly before your eyes. Too many of us settle down on a padded pew and become introverted. Our world becomes a monastery without walls. Our friendships are confined solely to people within the Church, but Jesus was the friend of sinners (see Matt. 11:19). So take the time to deliberately befriend the lost for the sake of their salvation. Remember that each and every person who dies in his sins has an appointment with the Judge of the universe. Hell opens wide its terrible jaws. There is no more sobering task than to be entrusted with the gospel of salvation—working with God for the eternal well-being of dying humanity. Have the same attitude as the apostle Paul, who pleaded that others would pray for his own personal witness. He said, "Pray also for me, that the message may be given to me when I open my mouth to make known with boldness the mystery of the gospel. For this I am an ambassador in chains. Pray that I might be bold enough in Him to speak as I should" (Eph. 6:19-20, *HCSB*).

4. PRAYER—"WAIT FOR A MINUTE"

God always answers prayer. Sometimes He says yes, sometimes He says no, and sometimes He says, "Wait for a minute." And because God is outside the dimension of time—and to Him a thousand years is no different than a day (see 2 Pet. 3:8)—that could mean a 10-year wait for us. So ask in faith, but rest in peace-filled patience.

Surveys show that over 90 percent of Americans pray daily. No doubt many pray for health, wealth, happiness, and the like. They also pray when Grandma gets sick, so when Grandma doesn't get better (or dies), many end up disillusioned or bitter. This is because they don't understand what the Bible says about prayer. God's Word teaches, among other things, that our sin will keep God from even hearing our prayers (Ps. 66:18), and that if we pray with doubt, we will not get an answer (Jas. 1:6-7). Here's how to be sure that you are heard:

- Pray with faith (see Heb. 11:6).
- Pray with clean hands and a pure heart (see Ps. 24:3-4).
- Pray genuine heartfelt prayers rather than vain repetitions (see Matt. 6:7).
- Make sure you are praying to the God revealed in the Holy Scriptures (see Exod. 20:3-6).

How Do We "Pray with Faith"?

Someone once said to me, "Ray, you're a man of great faith in God," thinking that he was paying me a compliment. But he was not—the compliment was due to God. For example, if I said, "I'm a man of great faith in my doctor," it's actually the doctor I'm complimenting. If I have great faith in my doctor, it means that I see him as a man of integrity, a man of great ability—I believe that he is trustworthy. I give glory to the man through my faith in him.

The Bible says that Abraham "did not waver at the promise of God through unbelief, but was strengthened in faith, giving glory to God, and being fully convinced that what He had promised He was also able to perform" (Rom. 4:20-21). Abraham was a man of great faith in God. Remember, that is not a compliment to Abraham. It is a compliment to God. Abraham had merely caught a glimpse of God's incredible ability, His impeccable integrity and His wonderful faithfulness to keep every promise He makes. Abraham's faith gave glory to a faithful God.

As far as God is concerned, if you belong to Jesus, you are a VIP. You are allowed to boldly come before the throne of grace (see Heb. 4:16). You have access to the King because you are the son or daughter of the King, and as such, you have the privilege to petition God in faith. When you were a child, did you have to grovel to get your needs met by your mom or dad? I hope not.

So don't pray, "Oh, God, I hope You will supply my needs." Instead, say something like, "Father, thank You that You keep every promise You make. Your Word says that you will supply all my needs according to Your riches in glory in Christ Jesus [see Phil. 4:19]. Therefore, I thank You that You will do this thing for my family. I ask this in the wonderful name of Jesus. Amen." Compare this to how Jesus prayed in John 11:42.

The great missionary Hudson Taylor said, "The prayer power has never been tried to its full capacity. If we want to see Divine power wrought in the place of weakness, failure, and disappointment, let us answer God's standing challenge, 'Call unto me, and I will answer you, and show you great and mighty things of which you know not of'" (Jer. 33:3).

How Do We Get "Clean Hands and a Pure Heart"?
We get clean hands and a pure heart simply by confessing our sins to God, through Jesus Christ, whose blood cleanses us from all our sin (see 1 John 1:7-9). God will not only forgive our every sin, but He also promises to forget our sins (see Heb. 8:12). He will consider us as though we had never sinned in the first place. He will make us pure in His sight—sinless. He will even purge our conscience so that we will no longer have a sense of guilt that we sinned. That's why we need to soak ourselves in Holy Scripture. Read the letters to the churches and see the wonderful things that God has done for us through the cross of Calvary. If we don't bother to read the "will," we will not have any idea what has been given to us.

How Do We Pray "Genuine Heartfelt Prayers"?

Our prayers will be genuine and heartfelt simply by keeping ourselves in the love of God. If the love of God is in us, we will never pray hypocritical or selfish prayers. In fact, we will not have to pray selfish prayers if we have a heart of love, because when our prayer life is pleasing to God, He will reward us openly (see Matt. 6:6). Just talk to your heavenly Father as candidly and intimately as a young child who is nestled on his daddy's lap would talk to his earthly father. How would you feel if every day your child pulled out a pre-written statement to dryly recite to you rather than pouring out the events and emotions of that day? God wants to hear from your heart.

How Do We Know We're Praying to "the God Revealed in Scripture"?

If you want to know who the God of the Scriptures is, study the Bible. Don't accept the image of God portrayed by the world, even though it appeals to the natural mind. A gentle, kind, Santa Claus figure who dispenses good things with no sense of justice or truth appeals to guilty sinners. Look to the thundering and lightning that came from Mount Sinai. Gaze at Jesus on the cross of Calvary, hanging in unspeakable agony because of the justice of a holy God. Such thoughts tend to banish idolatry.

5. WARFARE—PRAISE THE LORD AND PASS THE AMMUNITION

When you became a Christian, you stepped right into the heat of an age-old battle. You now have three enemies: the world, the flesh and the devil. Let's look at each of these resistant enemies.

Our first enemy is the world—the sinful, rebellious world system. The world loves the darkness and hates the light (see John 3:20) and is governed by "the prince of the power of the air" (Eph. 2:2). The Bible says that the Christian has escaped the corruption that is in the world through lust. Lust is unlawful desire and is the life's blood of the world—whether it be the lust for sexual gratification, for power, for money, for material things. Lust is a monster that will never be gratified, so don't feed it. It will grow bigger and bigger until it weighs heavily upon your back, and it will be the death of you (see Jas. 1:15).

There is nothing wrong with sex, power, money or material things, but when desire for these things becomes predominant, it becomes idolatry (see Col. 3:5). We are told, "Do not love the world or the things in the world. If anyone loves the world, the love of the Father is not in him" (1 John 2:15), and "Whoever therefore wants to be a friend of the world makes himself an enemy of God" (Jas. 4:4).

The second enemy is the devil, who is the "god of this age" (2 Cor. 4:4). He was our spiritual father before we joined the family of God (see John 8:44; Eph. 2:2). Jesus called the devil a thief who came to steal, kill and destroy (see John 10:10). The way to overcome the devil and his demons is to make sure that we are outfitted with the spiritual armor of God that is listed in Ephesians 6:10-18. Become intimately familiar with this armor. Sleep in it. Never take it off. Bind the sword to your hand so that you will never lose your grip on it. The reason for doing this brings us to the third enemy.

The third enemy is what the Bible calls the flesh. The flesh is our sinful nature. The domain for the battle is our mind. If we do not protect our mind, we will be attracted to the world and to all its sin. The mind is the control panel for the eyes and the ears and the center of our appetites. All sin begins in the heart, which is the source of our thoughts (see Prov. 4:23; Matt. 15:19). We think of sin before we commit it. James 1:15 warns that lust brings forth sin, and that sin, when it's conceived, brings forth death. Every day of life we have a choice. To sin or not to sin—that is the question. The answer to the question, though, is for us to have the fear of God. If we don't fear God, we will sin to our sinful heart's delight.

Did you know that God kills people? He killed one man for sexual sin (see Gen. 38:9-10), another man for being greedy (see Luke 12:15-21), and a husband and wife for telling one lie (see Acts 5:1-10). Knowledge of God's goodness—His righteous judgments against evil—should put the fear of God in us and help us not to indulge in sin.

If we know that the eye of the Lord is in every place, beholding the evil and the good, and that God will bring every work to judgment, we will live accordingly. Such weighty thoughts are valuable, for "by the fear of the Lord one departs from evil" (Prov. 16:6). Jesus said, "And I say to you, My friends, do not be afraid of those who kill the body, and after that have no more that they can do. But I will show you whom you should fear: Fear Him who, after He has killed, has power to cast [people] into hell; yes, I say to you, fear Him!" (Luke 12:4-5).

6. FELLOWSHIP—FLUTTER BY BUTTERFLY

Pray about where you should fellowship. Make sure that the church home you select calls sin what it is: sin. Do the leaders believe the promises of God? Are they loving? Does the pastor treat his wife with respect? Is he a man of the Word? Does he have a humble heart and a gentle spirit? Listen closely to his teaching. It should glorify God, magnify Jesus and edify the believer.

One evidence that you have been truly saved is that you will have a love for other Christians (see 1 John 3:14). You will want to fellowship with them. The old saying that "birds of a feather flock together" is true of Christians. You gather together for the breaking of bread (communion), for teaching from the Word and for fellowship. You share the same inspirations, illuminations, inclinations, temptations, aspirations, motivations and perspirations, because you are working together for the same thing: the furtherance of the kingdom of God on earth. This is why you attend church—not because you have to but because you want to.

Don't become a "spiritual butterfly." If you are flitting from church to church, how will your pastor know what type of spiritual food you are digesting? The Bible says that your shepherd is accountable to God for you (see Heb. 13:17), so make yourself known to your pastor, and submit to his leadership.

Pray for your pastor regularly. Pray also for his wife, his family and the church leaders. Being a pastor is no easy task. Most people don't realize how long it takes to prepare a fresh sermon each week. They don't appreciate the time that the pastor spends in prayer and in the study of the Word. If your pastor repeats a joke or a story, remember, he's human. So give him a great deal of grace and double honor. Never murmur about him. If you don't like something he has said, pray about it, then leave the issue with God. If that doesn't satisfy you, then leave the church rather than divide the congregation through murmuring and complaining. God hates those who cause division among believers (see Prov. 6:16-19).

7. THANKSGIVING—DO THE RIGHT THING

For the Christian every day should be Thanksgiving Day. We should be thankful even in the midst of problems. The apostle Paul said, "I am overcome with joy in all our afflictions" (2 Cor. 7:4, *HCSB*). He knew that God was working all things together for his good—even his trials (see Rom. 8:28).

Problems will come your way, because God will see to it personally that you grow as a Christian. He will allow storms in your life in order to send your roots deep into the soil of His Word. Problems also cause us to pray more. It's been well said that we will see more from our knees than we will on our tiptoes.

A man once watched a butterfly struggling to get out of its cocoon. In an effort to help it, he took a razor blade and carefully slit the edge of the cocoon. The butterfly escaped from its problem—but immediately died. It is God's way to let the butterfly struggle. Its struggle is what causes its tiny heart to beat fast, thus sending the life's blood into its wings.

Trials have their purpose. They are a cocoon in which we often find ourselves. They make us struggle; they bring us to our knees. It is there that the life's blood of faith in God helps us spread our wings.

Faith and thanksgiving are close friends. If you have faith in God, you will be thankful, because you know the Lord's loving hand is upon you even while you are in a lion's den. That will give you a deep sense of joy, which is the barometer of the depth of your faith in God. Let me give you an example. Imagine that I said I would give you one million dollars if you sent me an email. Of course, you don't believe I would give people that kind of money. But imagine that you did believe it, and that you knew 1,000 people who had sent me an email and had received their million dollars—no strings attached. More than that, you actually called me to verify my promise, and I assured you personally that I would keep my word. If you believed me, wouldn't you have joy? If you didn't believe me—no joy. The amount of joy you have would be a barometer of how much you believed my promise.

We have so much for which to be thankful. God has given us "exceedingly great and precious promises" (2 Pet. 1:4) that are "more to be desired . . . than gold" (Ps. 19:10). Do yourself a big favor: believe those promises and thank God continually for them so that your "joy may be full" (John 15:11).

8. WATER BAPTISM—SPRINKLE OR IMMERSE?

The Bible says, "Repent . . . and be baptized, each of you, in the name of Jesus Christ for the forgiveness of your sins" (Acts 2:38, HCSB). There is no question about whether you should be baptized. The questions are how, when and by whom?

It would seem clear from Scripture that those who were baptized were fully immersed in water. Here's one reason why: "John also was baptizing in Aenon near Salim, because there was much water there" (John 3:23). If John were merely sprinkling believers, he would have needed only a cupful of water. Baptism by immersion pictures our death to sin, our burial and our resurrection to new life in Christ (see Rom. 6:4; Col. 2:12).

The Philippian jailer and his family were baptized at midnight, the same hour that they believed (see Acts 16:30-33). The Ethiopian eunuch was baptized as soon as he believed (see 8:35-38), as was Paul (see 9:17-18). Baptism is a step of obedience, and God blesses our obedience. So what are you waiting for?

Who should baptize you? It is clear from Scripture that other believers had the privilege to do this, but check with your pastor; he may want the honor himself.

9. TITHING—THE FINAL FRONTIER

It has been said that the wallet is the "final frontier." It is the final area to be conquered—the last thing that we surrender to God. Jesus spoke much about money. He said that we cannot serve both God and mammon (see Matt. 6:24). The word used for "money" was the common Aramaic word for "riches," which is related to a Hebrew word signifying "that which is to be trusted." In other words, we cannot trust God and money. Either our source of joy, our great love, our sense of security, the supplier of our needs is money—or it is God.

When you open your purse or wallet, give generously and regularly to your local church. A guide to how much you should give can be found in the "tithe" of the Old Testament: 10 percent of your income. Whatever amount you give, make sure you give something to the work of God (see Mal. 3:8-11). Give because you want to, not because you have to. God loves a cheerful giver (see 2 Cor. 9:6-7), so learn to hold your money with a loose hand.

10. TROUBLESHOOTING: CULTS, ATHEISTS AND SKEPTICS

If you know the Lord, nothing will shake your faith. It is true that the man with an experience will never be at the mercy of a man with an argument. If you are converted and the Holy Spirit testifies within you that you are a child of God (see Rom. 8:16), you will never be shaken by a skeptic.

When cults tell you that to be saved you must call God by a certain name, or that you must worship on a certain day, or that an elder of their church must baptize you, don't panic. Merely go back to the Instruction Manual. The Bible has all the answers, and searching them out will make you grow. If you feel intimidated by atheists, thinking that they are intellectuals, read my book *God Doesn't Believe in Atheists*. It will reveal that atheists are the opposite of discerning. It will also show you how to prove God's existence and also to prove that the "atheist" does not exist.

Finally, you need to keep yourself fit. An athlete knows that the way to prevent sporting injury and pain is to stay in shape. Exercise spiritually, as the apostle Paul did. He said, "Herein do I exercise myself, to always have a conscience void of offense toward God, and toward men" (Acts 24:16, *KJV*). Do the same. Listen to the voice of your conscience. It's your friend, not your enemy. Remember the words of Solomon: "Fear God and keep His commands, for this is man's all. For God will bring every work into judgment, including every secret thing, whether good or evil" (Eccles. 12:13-14).

Keep the Day of Judgment before your eyes. On that day you will be glad that you cultivated a tender conscience. I hope these principles have been helpful and that they will someday save you some pain.

ENDNOTES

Chapter 1: Job and Tragedy

1. "What Happened Before the Big Bang?" (The Science Channel, July 14, 2011).
2. C. H. Spurgeon, "Job's Resignation," sermon #2457 delivered on March 11, 1886, the Metropolitan Tabernacle, Newington, UK.

Chapter 2: Job and Evil

1. Rob Brendle, "My Take: This Is Where God Was in Aurora," CNN Special, July 28, 2012. http://religion.blogs.cnn.com/category/church/page/2/.
2. Matthew Henry, *Matthew Henry's Concise Commentary on the Bible* (New York: Robert Carter and Brothers, 1856), Job 2:7-10.
3. C. H. Spurgeon, "Job's Resignation," sermon delivered March 11, 1886, Metropolitan Tabernacle, Newington, UK.
4. "How Many Bicyclists Are Killed and Injured Each Year," data from the National Highway Traffic Safety Administration, 2009 data. http://www.bicyclinginfo.org/faqs/answer.cfm?id=40

Chapter 3: Job and Karma

1. Stephanie Pappas, "Mass Shooting: Why It's So Hard to Predict Who Will Snap," FOX News, July 25, 2012. http://www.foxnews.com/health/2012/07/24/mass-shootings-why-it-so-hard-to-predict-who-will-snap/#ixzz21eeEMh5A.
2. Erika Christakis, "The Overwhelming Maleness of Mass Homicide," *TIME*.com, July 24, 2012. http://www.cnn.com/2012/07/24/opinion/christakis-males-homicide/index.html.
3. Norimitsu Onishi, "Lucas and Rich Neighbors Agree to Disagree: Part II," *The New York Times*, May 21, 2012. http://www.nytimes.com/2012/05/22/us/george-lucas-retreats-from-battle-with-neighbors.html.

Chapter 4: Job and Justice

1. "Wiesenthal Center Submits New Evidence of Crimes by Most Wanted Suspect Laszlo Csatary and Urges Hungarian Prosecutors to Put the Former Senior Police Officer on Trial in Budapest," The Simon Wiesenthal Center, July 15, 2012. http://www.wiesenthal.com/site/apps/nlnet/content2.aspx?c=lsKWLbPJLnF&b=4441467&ct=12011929#.UR0v3-jeT8A.

Chapter 5: Job and Tough Questions

1. Jeffrey Kluger, "Life in the Universe: Easy or Hard?" *TIME*, May 14, 2012. http://newsfeed.time.com/2012/05/14/life-in-the-universe-easy-or-hard/.
2. Andrew Moseman, "The Estimated Number of Stars in the Universe Just Tripled," Discover, December 1, 2010. http://blogs.discovermagazine.com/80beats/2010/12/01/the-estimated-number-of-stars-in-the-universe-just-tripled/.
3. Charles Q. Choi, "Discovery May Triple the Number of Stars in the Universe," Space.com. http://www.space.com/9625-discovery-triple-number-stars-universe.html.
4. Albert Einstein, quoted in Rich Deem, "Did Einstein Believe in a Personal God?" Evidence for God. http://www.godandscience.org/apologetics/einstein.html.

Chapter 6: Job, the Hand-made Man

1. "What Is Hair?" Pantene.com. http://pantene.com/en-US/hair-science/pages/what-is-hair.aspx.

2. Richard Dawkins, *The Blind Watchmaker* (New York: W. W. Norton & Company, 1996), p. 1.
3. Ray Comfort, *You Can Lead an Atheist to Evidence, but You Can't Make Him Think: Answers to Questions from Angry Skeptics* (Washington, DC: WND Books, 2009).

Chapter 7: Job and the Law

1. Rob Preece, "Why Criminals Believe in Heaven: People Who Trust in Redemption More Likely to Break the Law than Those Who Think There's a Hell," Mail Online, June 23, 2012. http://www.dailymail.co.uk/sciencetech/article-2163771/Why-criminals-believe-heaven-Study-finds-crime-rates-vary-according-religious-beliefs.html#ixzz1yyi39vuQ.
2. C. S. Lewis, *Mere Christianity* (New York: HarperCollins, 2007), pp. 35-36.
3. Martin Johnston, "Eight Glasses of Water a Day? No, Says Expert," *The New Zealand Herald*, June 7, 2012. http://www.nzherald.co.nz/lifestyle/news/article.cfm?c_id=6&objectid=10811310.
4. See "Ray Comfort on the Carol Lieberman Show." http://www.youtube.com/watch?v=4FhXIvB96tc&feature=related.

Chapter 9: Job and Moral Relativism

1. Mike Osler, "My Take: The Christian Cause for Gay Marriage," CNN, May 19, 2012. http://religion.blogs.cnn.com/2012/05/19/my-take-the-christian-case-for-gay-marriage/.
2. Wendy Geller, "Carrie Underwood Supports Gay Marriage," Yahoo Music Blogs, June 11, 2012. http://music.yahoo.com/blogs/our-country/carrie-underwood-supports-gay-marriage-001952640.html.

Chapter 10: Job and Messianic Prophecy

1. Ray Comfort, *The Evidence Bible* (Gainesville, FL: Bridge-Logos, 2003).
2. "Fulfilled Messianic Prophecies (So Far)," PreservedWords.com. http://www.preservedwords.com/prophecies.htm.
3. Matthew Henry, *Matthew Henry's Concise Commentary on the Bible* (New York: Robert Carter and Brothers, 1856), Genesis 3:15.

Chapter 12: Job and Idolatry

1. A.W. Tozer, *The Knowledge of the Holy* (San Francisco: HarperOne, 1978).
2. This tract is available through www.livingwaters.com.
3. Catherine Mumford Booth, "Godliness: How to Work for God with Success," *Papers on Godliness* (London, John Snow & Co., 1896), p. 110.
4. C. H. Spurgeon, "His Name—the Mighty God," sermon #258 delivered on July 19, 1859, at the Music Hall, Royal Surrey Gardens, London, UK.

Chapter 13: Job and Trust

1. John Bunyan, *Pilgrim's Progress* (London: Cassell, Petter & Galpin, 1864), p. 6.
2. Soledad O'Brien, *Starting Point* transcript, *CNN*, June 27, 2012. http://transcripts.cnn.com/TRANSCRIPTS/1206/27/sp.01.html.
3. For more information on dealing with panic attacks, see my book *Overcoming Panic Attacks* (Gainesville, FL: Bridge-Logos, 2005).
4. Megan O'Matz, "Tomas Lopez Lifeguard on *TODAY* Show: Hallandale Lifeguard Firing by Jeff Ellis Management on *TODAY*," *Sun Sentinel*, July 5, 2012. http://www.wptv.com/dpp/news/state/tomas-lopez-lifeguard-on-today-show-hallandale-lifeguard-firing-by-jeff-ellis-management-on-today#ixzz1zkrkDx4Y.
5. Published with permission.
6. Theodore Cuylar (1822–1909), "Words of Cheer for Christian Pilgrims." Cuylar was an American Presbyterian minister and writer who graduated from Princeton University in 1841.

Chapter 14: Job and Scientific Truths

1. Matthew Henry, *Matthew Henry's Concise Commentary on the Bible* (New York: Robert Carter and Brothers, 1856), Job 26:1-14.
2. Ibid.
3. A layer of permeable rock, sand, or gravel through which ground water flows, containing enough water to supply wells and springs.
4. "When Was the Water Cycle Discovered?" Answers.com. http://wiki.answers.com/Q/When_was_the_water_cycle_discovered.

Chapter 15: Job and Lust

1. Matthew Henry, *Matthew Henry's Concise Commentary on the Bible* (New York: Robert Carter and Brothers, 1856), Job 31:1-40.

Chapter 16: Job and "If"

1. Adam Clarke, *Clarke's Commentary on the Bible* (New York: J. Emory and B. Waugh, 1831), Job 31:1.
2. In the U.S., there are about 200 to 300 new cases diagnosed per year, with most coming from exposures during foreign travel. The majority of worldwide cases are found in the tropics or subtropics (for example, Brazil, India and Indonesia). The WHO reports about 500,000 to 700,000 new cases per year worldwide, with curing of about 14 million cases since 1985. http://www.medicinenet.com/leprosy/page6.htm.

Chapter 17: Job and Water

1. Katia Moskvitch, "Moon 'Too Dry to Have Life,' Say Scientists," Discovery News, August 5, 2010.
2. Kristina Grifantini, "Where Did Earth's Water Come From?" Life's Little Mysteries, July 13, 2011. http://www.lifeslittlemysteries.com/1596-where-did-water-come-from.html.
3. C. Robert Reszka, Jr., "Where Does 'New Water' Come From?" AllExperts, October 25, 2009. http://en.allexperts.com/q/Geology-1359/2009/10/new-water-2.htm.
4. Ibid.
5. That number includes all natural lakes, but not human-made lakes such as reservoirs formed by dams. See Liz Osborn, "Number of Lakes in the World," Current Results. http://www.currentresults.com/Environment-Facts/number-lakes-in-world.php.

Chapter 18: Job and the Wonders of Creation

1. C. H. Spurgeon, "Job Among the Ashes," sermon #2009 delivered on February 19, 1888, at the Metropolitan Tabernacle, Newington, UK.
2. Steven A. Austin, "Springs of the Ocean," Institute for Creation Research, *Acts & Facts*, vol. 10, no. 8. http://www.icr.org/article/springs-ocean/.
3. "Wilson A. Bentley: The Snowflake Man," Snowflake Bentley. http://snowflakebentley.com/bio.htm.
4. "VLF Emissions are Natural Radio signals that are thought to originate in the magnetosphere on the sunward side of the earth near the geomagnetic equator and then propagate toward the poles along the field lines where they exit the ionosphere and propagate along the surface of the earth where they may be heard." http://naturalradiolab.com/content/view/22/24/.
5. "Earth Songs," NASA Science News, January 19, 2001. http://science.nasa.gov/science news/science-at-nasa/2001/ast19jan_1/.

Chapter 19: Job and the Holocaust

1. "Val Patterson: Obituary (1953–2012)," *Salt Lake Tribune*. http://www.legacy.com/obituaries/saltlaketribune/obituary.aspx?pid=158526785#fbLoggedOut.

Chapter 20: Job and the Dinosaur

1. Paleontologists use the term "sauropod" to describe large, four-legged, plant-eating dinosaurs with bulky trunks, long necks and tails, and tiny heads with small brains. The name *sauropod* is Greek for "lizard foot," which was among these dinosaurs' least distinctive traits. See Bob Strauss, "Sauropods—The Biggest Dinosaurs," About.com. http://dinosaurs.about.com/od/typesofdinosaurs/a/sauropods.htm.

2. Bob Strauss, "The 10 Biggest Dinosaurs," About.com. http://dinosaurs.about.com/od/typesofdinosaurs/tp/Five-Biggest-Dinosaurs.htm.

3. "'Thunder-Thighs' Dinosaur Discovered: Brontomerus May Have Used Powerful Thigh Muscles to Kick Predators," ScienceDaily, February 23, 2011. http://www.sciencedaily.com/releases/2011/02/110223071203.htm.

4. Ethan Schowaiter-Hay, "How Big Do Cedar Trees Get in Diameter?" eHow. http://www.ehow.com/facts_7784614_big-do-cedar-trees-diameter.html

5. "15 Things You Didn't Know About Dinosaurs," Dino Don's Dinosaur World. http://www.dinodon.com/15facts.htm

6. Dave Miller, "The 'First of the Ways of God,'" Apologetics Press. http://www.apologeticspress.org/apcontent.aspx?category=9&article=2417

7. "Supersaurus," Enchanted Learning. http://www.enchantedlearning.com/subjects/dinosaurs/dinos/Supersaurus.shtml.

8. D. L. Parsell, "Mass Extinction That Led to Age of Dinosaurs Was Swift, Study Shows," National Geographic News, May 10, 2001. http://news.nationalgeographic.com/news/2001/05/0510_massex.html.

9. Stefan Anitei, "What Caused Dinosaur Extinction?" Stoftpedia, October 31, 2006. http://news.softpedia.com/news/What-Caused-Dinosaurs-039-Extinction-39017.shtml.

10. "Dinosaurs 'Gassed' Themselves into Extinction, British Scientists Say," FOX News, May 7, 2012. http://www.foxnews.com/scitech/2012/05/07/dinosaurs-farted-their-way-to-extinction-british-scientists-say/.

Chapter 21: Job and the Future

1. C. S. Lewis, *The Screwtape Letters,* published in Walter Hooper, *C. S. Lewis: A Complete Guide to His Life and Work* (New York: HarperCollins, 1996), p. 269.

2. John MacArthur, "A Colossal Fraud," Grace to You, December 7, 2009. http://www.gty.org/Blog/B091207.

3. Katherine Schulten, "How Do You Define 'Family'?" The Learning Network, February 24, 2011. http://learning.blogs.nytimes.com/2011/02/24/how-do-you-define-family/.

4. Ramon Johnson, "Gay Population Statistics," 2011. http://gaylife.about.com/od/comingout/a/population.htm.

5. Lyman Morales, "U.S. Adults Estimate that 25 percent of Americans Are Gay or Lesbian," Gallup Politics, May 27, 2011. http://www.gallup.com/poll/147824/adults-estimate-americans-gay-lesbian.aspx.

6. Sarah Aarthun, "Chick-fil-A Wades into Fast-food Fight Over Same-sex Marriage Rights," CNN, July 28, 2012.

7. "Are Earthquakes Really on the Increase?" USGS. http://earthquake.usgs.gov/learn/topics/increase_in_earthquakes.php.

8. Deanna Conners, "Are Large Earthquakes Increasing in Frequency?" EarthSky, March 4, 2012. http://earthsky.org/earth/are-large-earthquakes-increasing-in-frequency.

9. "War and Conflict," Global Issues Overview. http://www.worldrevolution.org/projects/globalissuesoverview/overview2/PeaceNew.htm.

10. "Lawlessness"—a reference to the moral Law.

11. "Marriage Obsolete? Four in 10 Say Yes," *The Huffington Post,* November 18, 2010. http://www.huffingtonpost.com/2010/11/18/marriage-obsolete-four-in_n_785482.html.

12. Ibid.

13. Channing Walker, "Overcrowded Prisons: What to Do?" *The Christian Science Monitor,* May 21, 2012. http://www.csmonitor.com/The-Culture/Articles-on-Christian-Science/2012/0521/Overcrowded-prisons-what-to-do.

14. Adam Gopnik, "The Caging of America: Why Do We Lock Up So Many People?" *The New Yorker,* January 30, 2012. http://www.newyorker.com/arts/critics/atlarge/2012/01/30/120130crat_atlarge_gopnik.

15. "Poll: In a Changing Nation, Santa Endures," NBC News, December 22, 2006. http://www.msnbc.msn.com/id/16329025/ns/us_news-life/t/poll-changing-nation-santa-endures/.

16. "Fable," Dictionary.com. http://dictionary.reference.com/browse/fable?s=t.

17. "Worldwide Flu Pandemic Strikes: 1918–1919," PBS. http://www.pbs.org/wgbh/aso/databank/entries/dm18fl.html.

18. "HIV/AIDS Facts," Greater than One. http://greaterthanone.org/about/hivaids-facts.html.

19. Saundra Young, "Talk of 'Cure' at Historic AIDS Conference," CNN, July 24, 2012. http://www.cnn.com/2012/07/23/health/hiv-aids-conference.

20. "World Cancer Day: Global Action to Avert 8 Million Cancer-related Deaths by 2015," World Heath Organization, February 3, 2006. http://www.who.int/mediacentre/news/releases/2006/pr06/en/index.html.

21. Wynne Parry, "7 Devastating Infectious Diseases," Live Science, April 13, 2011. http://www.livescience.com/13694-devastating-infectious-diseases-smallpox-plague.html.

22. Ken Ham and Tim Lovett, "Was There Really a Noah's Ark and Flood?" Answersingenesis.org, October 11. 2007. http://www.answersingenesis.org/articles/nab/really-a-flood-and-ark.

23. "Is Marriage Still Relevant?" BBC News, December 3, 2011. http://news.bbc.co.uk/2/hi/talking_point/1678523.stm.

24. "Marriage Obsolete? Four in 10 Say Yes," *The Huffington Post.*

25. "Famine Threat to 15m: Ethiopia PM," CNN World, November 12, 2002. http://edition.cnn.com/2002/WORLD/africa/11/11/ethiopia.famine/.

26. "Millions Facing Famine in Ethiopia as Rains Fail," *The Independent,* August 30, 2009. http://www.independent.co.uk/news/world/africa/millions-facing-famine-in-ethiopia-as-rains-fail-1779376.html.

27. "10 Million Face Famine in West Africa," *The Independent,* May 30, 2010. http://www.independent.co.uk/news/world/africa/10-million-face-famine-in-west-africa-1986875.html.

28. Jeffrey Gettleman, "U.N. Officials Say Famine Is Widening in Somalia," *The New York Times,* September 5, 2011. http://www.nytimes.com/2011/09/06/world/africa/06somalia.html.

29. "Vegetarianism in America," Vegetarian Times. http://www.vegetariantimes.com/article/vegetarianism-in-america/.

30. Andrew Joseph, "Jerusalem Is at the Center of Another Conflict: Separation of Powers," *The Atlantic,* November 8, 2011. http://www.theatlantic.com/international/archive/2011/11/jerusalem-is-at-the-center-of-another-conflict-separation-of-powers/248079/.

31. "Jordanian Bomber of CIA Base Deceived Family," *Oregon Herald,* January 5, 2010. http://www.oregonherald.com/news/show-story.cfm?id=103618.

32. Erick Stakelbeck, "Israel Allies to US: Recognize Jerusalem as Capital," CBN News, June 10, 2012. http://www.cbn.com/cbnnews/insideisrael/2012/June/Caucus-to-US-Acknowledge-Jerusalem-as-Israels-Capital/.

33. "Israel Prepared for Attack," The Jewish Reporter, May 23, 2012. http://thejewish reporter.com/2012/05/23/israel-prepares-for-attack/.

34. Joanna Paraszczuk, "Ahmadinejad: World Forces Must Annihilate Israel," *The Jerusalem Post,* August 2, 2012. http://www.jpost.com/IranianThreat/News/Article.aspx?id= 279864.

35. "Leadership for a Changing World," Darren Hardy. http://darrenhardy.success.com/ 2011/03/changing-world/.

36. Matthew Henry, *Matthew Henry's Concise Commentary on the Bible* (New York: Robert Carter and Brothers, 1856), notes on 2 Peter 3:4.

37. Flavius Josephus, *The Wars of the Jews or History of the Destruction of Jerusalem,* bk. VII, 1.1.

38. Henry Hart Milman, *The History of the Jews,* book 16 (London: George Routledge and Sons, 1878).

39. Adapted from "Battle for Jerusalem (19848), Wikipedia.org. http://en.wikipedia.org/ wiki/Battle_for_Jerusalem_(1948).

Epilogue: Save Yourself Some Pain

1. Hector Tobar, "Fire in Converted Watts Garage Kills 5 Children," *Los Angeles Times,* December 20, 1996. http://articles.latimes.com/1996-12-20/news/mn-11040_1_ converted-garage.

For many free resources and other books from the ministry of Ray Comfort, please check out:

WWW.LIVINGWATERS.COM

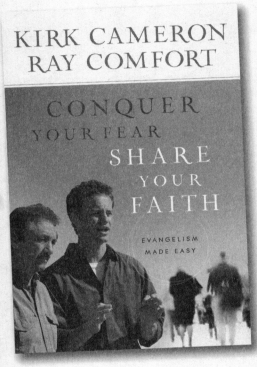

DISCOVER THE SECRETS BEHIND THE SMILE...

STILL GROWING

kirk cameron

Kirk Cameron is best known for his role as loveable teenage troublemaker Mike Seaver on the award-winning TV series *Growing Pains*, but his rise to fame and fortune is only part of his incredible story. In this intimate autobiography, Kirk opens up about his early years, his rocket to stardom, his life-changing encounter with Jesus and the hard choices he's made along the way to live in the Way of the Master. You will get an up-close look at what drives the former teen-magazine heartthrob and find out how God and family became the secrets behind his celebrated smile. In his own words, Kirk shares how he's still growing—even through the triumphs and temptations of his Hollywood career.

Still Growing: An Autobiography
Kirk Cameron
with Lissa Halls Johnson
ISBN 978-08307-4451-0